50
PLANTS
THAT YOU
CAN'T KILL

First published in Great Britain in 2019 by Mitchell Beazley
an imprint of Octopus Publishing Group Limited
Carmelite House
50 Victoria Embankment
London EC4Y 0DZ
www.octopusbooks.co.uk

An Hachette UK Company
www.hachette.co.uk

Published in association with the Royal Horticultural Society
Copyright © 2019 Quarto Publishing plc

A CIP record for this is available from the British Library

ISBN 978-1-78472-589-1

This book was conceived, designed and produced by
The Bright Press, an imprint of the Quarto Group
6 Blundell Street
London N7 9BH

RHS Publisher: Rae Spencer-Jones
RHS Editor: Simon Maughan
Head of Editorial: Chris Young

Publisher: Mark Searle
Creative Director: James Evans
Art Director: Katherine Radcliffe
Managing Editor: Jacqui Sayers
Editor: Abbie Sharman
Designer: Grade Design, gradedesign.com

10 9 8 7 6 5 4 3 2 1

Printed in Slovenia by GPS Group

The Royal Horticultural Society is the UK's
leading gardening charity dedicated to
advancing horticulture and promoting good
gardening. Its charitable work includes
providing expert advice and information,
training the next generation of gardeners,
creating hands-on opportunities for children
to grow plants and conducting research
into plants, pests and environmental issues
affecting gardeners.

For more information visit www.rhs.org.uk
or call 0845 130 4646.

Image note:
The image on the opening spread for each
plant is an image of the main plant, not of
the variations in the 'others to try' box.

50
PLANTS
THAT YOU
CAN'T KILL

SUREFIRE PLANTS TO GROW
INDOORS AND OUT

Jamie Butterworth

MITCHELL
BEAZLEY

CONTENTS

FRUITS AND VEGETABLES

HOUSE PLANTS

INTRODUCTION

First things first: no plant is truly unkillable, but there are many plants that are stubborn and resilient. This book will introduce you to the tough side of the plant world and show you a range of plants that just don't know when to quit.

Within this book are 50 plants that I personally believe are foolproof options that will show you that you're not as bad a gardener as you once thought. These amazing plants are at the shallow end of the gardening pool and are the ideal starter plants to get going with. The key to success with any garden is making sure you choose the right plants for the right place. From perennials to shrubs, house plants to vegetables, there is something for everyone, and for every garden.

Don't underestimate plants. Plants and gardens can help you live longer: people that live on tree-lined streets are scientifically proven to live longer; people that surround themselves with greenery live longer; people that get down and dirty with plants and soil are healthier, happier and, you guessed it, live longer.

Gardens become an escape from our day-to-day troubles, somewhere to switch off and reconnect with nature. The act of embracing plants and gardens has a wholesome goodness attached to it, an enriching process that frees up your mind and allows you to switch off. Something we should all do more of.

Despite being so good for you, gardening is often seen as something that should be left to your grandparents, but rest assured that you don't need a bus pass or a degree in Latin to pick up a trowel. Anyone and everyone can garden, no matter how old you are, where you are from, what you do for a living or how much you earn. Gardening is fun, exciting and rewarding, and is so much more than simply cutting the lawn or doing a bit of weeding.

Once you've sown your first seeds and watched them germinate, grow and flower, I challenge you not to be hooked. It truly is one of life's simplest, easiest and most genuine pleasures, to create something from nothing. It also costs very little, which always helps.

Plants have adapted over millennia to grow and thrive in the toughest of conditions across the world. However, every plant, no matter how tough, requires a modicum of love. This doesn't mean it has to become life-consuming and over-demanding; but a little water, time and affection can go a long way to keeping your plants alive. Follow the simple and easy planting advice within this book and you'll be blessed with a flourishing garden (or windowsill). Roll up your sleeves, get your hands dirty and get stuck in!

SOURCING AND BUYING PLANTS

Plant shopping can be a fun and rewarding experience. On a sunny spring day, there is nothing better than having a leisurely wander through a local nursery to choose plants that will festoon your garden and bring enjoyment for months and years to come.

When buying plants, it is important to purchase from reputable, quality growers. There are thousands of small, independent, local plant nurseries, each a fount of knowledge and a great source of inspiration. These shops are often passed from generation to generation, so they are the perfect place for advice and ideas.

Choosing healthy, well-grown plants is key to success. You want to avoid buying any plant that has become root-bound (the roots are beginning to bulge out of the pot), and equally any plants that have only recently been potted and there is a lot of loose compost. If you take the plant out of the pot, the roots should be visible, but not congested.

Avoid buying plants that look stressed, or have visible damage, pests or diseases. Although long term they will most likely be fine, buying healthy plants will give you a great head start. Equally, don't be tempted to just fill your trolley with plants already in flower; they will probably only last for a few more weeks and then start to die back. Buy plants when young, fresh and keen, and allow them to do the growing and flowering in your own garden for maximum enjoyment.

If you have any specific plant queries or want further advice on what would work best in your particular garden, go in and speak to one of the expert growers. Gardeners are lovely people, and will rejoice in sharing information, tips and tricks with you.

POTS AND CONTAINERS

It is perfectly possible to have an amazing garden without having much space. In fact, I myself only tend to be able to grow plants within containers due to the lack of a sizeable garden. This is the perfect solution for anyone with just a patio, balcony or small space that needs an injection of colour, but who doesn't have the luxury of large beds to grow their plants in.

This book will feature not only easy-to-grow plants that will bring life into your garden, but plants that will thrive when grown in a container or pot. As long as the container is big enough and attention is given to their care, it is possible to grow any plant in a container, from spring bulbs to statement shrubs and everything in between.

When choosing a container, the sky really is the limit. It can be anything from a terracotta pot to a kitchen sink. Be fun, inventive and make it your own. The style of the container should ideally match the feel of the garden you are hoping to create. The price of your container can vary massively depending on the size and the material it is made from, so if you are on a tight budget, trying getting creative and upcycling and recycling.

The key is to ensure that whatever you choose has good drainage. If your container of choice doesn't already benefit from drainage holes, add some yourself by carefully drilling a few holes into its base. Add a layer of broken crockery to the base to aid with drainage, and fill with a good multipurpose compost.

Growing plants in containers is no different from growing plants in the ground, only you may have to water and feed more regularly. Plants will typically grow smaller in a container than they would in the ground, but this is no bad thing, especially in a smaller garden. Keep a close eye on your pots, especially during the summer months, as containers can dry out very quickly during warm spells. Using a mulch on the surface of the compost can help retain some moisture.

The added benefit to growing plants within containers is that you have the advantage of being able to lift and move the container to a new location; this can be useful if the plants do not seem to be enjoying where they are. A movable garden is also ideal if you live in rented accommodation, as the plants can follow you on your journey and continue to bring enjoyment.

WATERING AND FEEDING

This may seem basic, but it is the number one cause of plant fatalities. All plants need water; even the ones that don't need much water still need some water. Lack of watering for weeks on end during hot, sunny spells is guaranteed to result in the garden becoming a plant crematorium.

Watering really is simple but can easily become overcomplicated. The key is to make sure the water is getting to the roots, as this is where the moisture will be collected and dispersed to the rest of the plant. Simply spraying the foliage won't do much to help the plant.

Watering is plant and location dependent; there is no fixed formula for determining how often or how much you should be watering. You should be aiming to water once the soil has begun to dry out. The best way to check this is to put your finger in the ground to see how wet it is. If you can feel moisture, leave it alone, but if it is dry, get the watering can out.

Try to water in the mornings and evenings when you can. Although this is not always possible, doing this will help you to avoid wasting water due to evaporation or causing the plant to scorch where the water droplets cook in the heat of the day.

Just like humans, plants need water and food to survive. Granted, they're not looking for an occasional chocolate bar, but they do need key nutrients to enable them to grow and thrive. A lack of any of these nutrients can cause the plant to become sickly and potentially die. Healthy, strong plants are much more likely to be able to withstand attacks from pests or diseases, making them harder to kill – and they will look better, too. There are two quick and easy methods for getting nutrients into your plants:

Liquid food (concentrated seaweed) – Seaweed is an organic, natural and fantastic fertiliser to use on your plants. It already contains all of the key 'ingredients' that plants need to establish and grow. Simply pour the liquid into your watering can and mix it into your water once a week, then water your plants as usual. No special mixing, measuring or worrying is required. Regular liquid feeding throughout the spring and summer can really help the plants do well.

Granular fertiliser – Granular fertilisers can be applied around the base of plants, especially during autumn and spring. They should be loosely dispersed around the base and then lightly raked into the soil. There are many different granular fertilisers available, and for specific requirements it is best to speak to your local nursery or garden centre for advice. For a general food, look for a balanced fertiliser that has a 7:7:7 ratio of the three key nutrients, nitrogen, potassium, and phosphorus; each of these is key to keeping plants healthy and flowering.

GET TO KNOW YOUR PLOT

The secret to growing plants is planting the right plant in the right place. To understand which plants you can or can't grow, you need to determine what conditions you have. Every garden is unique, with its own micro-climate, ideal for some plants and deadly for others. You can't do much to change these conditions, so you need to work with what you have.

The first thing to consider is aspect. What direction does your garden face? By this, I mean considering the direction the sun comes into the garden. By embracing the light levels and aspect you have, you can begin to plan accordingly and grow the plants that will best match the conditions you have. A compass can enable you to determine this.

South facing – These gardens typically benefit from large amounts of sun, resulting in heat traps, especially during the summer months. South facing gardens can be brilliant for sun- and dry-loving plants, allowing them to bask in the maximum amount of sunshine available.

North facing – These gardens tend to be shadier, with potentially no direct sunlight, which leads to a cooler garden. If this is you, do not despair, there are many shade loving plants that will thrive in these conditions and would simply dry out in a sunnier spot.

West facing – The ideal compromise between two extremes and arguably the perfect position, benefiting from shade during the morning and sun during the afternoon and evening. Perfect for plants that prefer a combination of both sun and shade. It is also a great spot for watching the sun set over the garden.

East facing – The opposite to a West facing garden, benefiting from sun during the morning and then shade during the afternoon and evening. Although it can be lovely to watch the sun rise, just be careful if growing anything delicate in an east-facing garden, as the morning sun can heat the dew on plant leaves, causing them to become slightly scorched.

One additional thing to consider is how exposed or sheltered your garden is. This too can play a part in choosing which plants will grow best in the space you have. A sheltered spot becomes ideal for tender plants, whereas an exposed position can be good for grasses and tough perennials that can withstand an occasional beating.

CHOPPING AND CHANGING

After growing a plant for a whole year, it may seem counterproductive to take the shears to it. However, it is in the interest of the plant to keep it well maintained and in check.

Plants are resilient, they don't want to die, and even if you get it wrong it is unlikely to be detrimental to the life of the plant. Yes, it may become ugly for a short period of time but most perennials and shrubs will spring back in a few months.

It is prudent to check with the RHS website before pruning. There are 12 pruning groups in total that cover every plant, so if you're at all uncertain, check first.

When you start pruning any plant, no matter whether it's a tree, shrub or perennial, you should always try and remove the four Ds. These are as follows:

Dead – Any dead growth within the plant can be removed to prevent any diseases from entering through the dead material.

Diseased – Any material that isn't right and is suffering from a disease.

Damaged – Any growth that has become damaged should be removed. Damaged growth can easily become a possible starting location for an infection or disease.

Duplicated – This mainly applies to large shrubs and trees and refers to any branches that have begun to rub and cross over one another. Branches crossing can cause weakness and, over time, result in disease.

Here are a few more terms that you may need, along with a quick introduction to what each one means:

Deadheading – A process in which you remove any spent and dead flower heads from the plant. By doing this, you can help encourage the plant to flower for longer.

Cutting back – This is a task for the winter months. This involves cutting perennials back to ground level. As herbaceous perennials will grow and flower in one year, then die back over the winter, they often leave behind the skeleton and structure. In many cases, this can be beautiful, especially in a heavy frost or morning dew. For this reason, I often leave these over winter and cut the plant right back to ground level in late February.

Chelsea chop – The best time to do this is the third week of May. This process involves cutting back herbaceous perennials by half. By doing this, you create a more compact, stronger plant that will produce more flowers over a longer period.

Pruning – There are dozens of books and websites that will go through this in lots of detail. These will advise on the best time of year, where to cut and what to cut.

PLANT TERMINOLOGY

Latin can be scary and off-putting. To grow plants and enjoy gardening, you do not need to be fluent in Latin or able to correctly identify every plant that has ever existed. Gardening is so much more than perplexing names, so relax and have fun in the garden.

Within this book, you will find that I have included the Latin names for the plants above the common names. Although the common names can be easier to remember and understand, they can also be associated with more than one plant, so I have included both names to avoid confusion. The Latin name is the universal way to identify that particular plant anywhere in the world and can be broken down into four parts. These are as follows:

Family – The family that the plant belongs to. This can help you understand which conditions the plant may or may not thrive in.

Genus – This is the main name for the plant and is most commonly used. Think of this as the plant's surname.

Species – Every plant has its own species, a subcategory of the genus that differentiates different plants within one group.

Cultivar – Cultivars are the fun names at the end; these tend to be the unique names given to the plant by whomever discovered or developed it. These can often be descriptive and give you an idea as to what the plant does. Cultivars tend to be bred to be more colourful, more scented, easier to grow or generally improved in some way.

There are several descriptive terms that categorize the life span and growth of the plant, so you know roughly what to expect when growing it.

Annual – A plant that germinates, grows, flowers and dies all in one year, these are typically started off from seed.

Biennial – A plant that typically lives for just two years, growing from seed in its first year and flowering in its second.

Perennial – A plant that comes back year after year. Most commonly these will die back during the winter months and bounce back in the spring, after a period of rest. Although perennials come back year after year, they can become tired after four or five years and need replacing or dividing (but not always).

Shrubs – A largely woody plant that grows bigger than a perennial. They often grow to

between one metre and three metres tall. These plants tend to be bushy and have multiple stems.

Trees – A tree is the largest of the plants and is typically anything that grows higher than three metres tall. A tree will have a main trunk, unlike a shrub.

Evergreen – A plant that keeps its leaves all year round.

Deciduous – A plant that loses its foliage during the winter months and grows fresh, new leaves the following spring.

10

PERENNIALS

THAT YOU
CAN'T KILL

AGAPANTHUS (AFRICAN LILY)

Trumpets are formed in large clusters held aloft by strong stems erupting out of clumps of leathery green foliage. Each plant can produce dozens of flowers during the summer, putting on a real firework-style display. The structure of the flowers can be appreciated both outdoors and in, as *Agapanthus* make a good cut flower for the house in vases and displays.

AGAPANTHUS
'NAVY BLUE'
AGAPANTHUS
▼

NEED TO KNOW

—

SIZE
UP TO 1M (3FT) TALL

—

LIGHT
FULL SUN

—

SOIL TYPE
SAND, CLAY, CHALK
OR LOAM

—

MOISTURE
MOIST BUT WELL
DRAINED

—

VARIETIES
A. 'Navy Blue';
A. 'Silver Baby';
A. *campanulatus* var.
albidus, white bell;
A. 'Black Buddhist'

WHY GROW IT

Agapanthus is a great addition to the garden. The bold and impressive flowers make a really powerful statement, adding drama and excitement to displays. Deciduous *Agapanthus* are generally tolerant of cold winters, despite their Mediterranean appearance, which also means they are very tough during summer heatwaves.

WHERE TO PUT IT

Some plants tolerate being grown in pots and containers but *Agapanthus* adores it. The container can actually help to encourage flowering, by restricting the roots and preventing the plant from focusing its energy just on foliage growth. The added benefit of growing in containers is that you can move the plants to a sheltered spot during the winter months, when *Agapanthus* can become vulnerable to frost damage. If planting directly into the ground, choose an open, sunny and exposed spot with good drainage.

HOW TO LOOK AFTER IT

The key to ensuring successional and continuous flowering is to keep the plants well fed. It takes a lot of energy to produce such an abundance of large flowers, so feed the plants every other week with a balanced liquid feed. Water regularly, especially during the drier months. For added protection during the winter months, try adding compost, bark or straw around the crown for extra defence from severe frosts.

DO

Grow in full sun where the hot temperatures can bake the ground

Mulch clumps during the winter months to help protect them from frost damage

Keep deadheading the flowers to keep the plant looking tidy – they also look great in a bouquet

DON'T

Be impatient – sometimes it can take up to three years for clumps to flower

Let the plants dry out – despite being extremely drought-tolerant, they need moisture in order to flower

Allow plants being grown in pots to become too root-bound – although they do prefer being compact, they still need room to grow and breathe

THREE TO TRY

01

01. *AGAPANTHUS CAMPANULATUS VAR. ALBIDUS*
WHITE BELL AGAPANTHUS
A pure-white deciduous *Agapanthus* that grows to around 60cm (24in) tall. The white flowers are born out of lush green foliage and are great left on the plant over winter.

02. *AGAPANTHUS* 'SILVER BABY'
A smaller-growing, deciduous *Agapanthus* that only grows to around 60cm (24in) tall, making it ideal if you have a smaller garden.

03. *AGAPANTHUS* 'BLACK BUDDHIST'
The deepest and darkest of all the *Agapanthus*, deciduous and fully hardy, with midnight black buds that open to reveal deep-blue trumpets that age well.

02

03

LADY'S MANTLE

Often, when choosing plants for the garden, it is all too easy to jump straight for those that produce an abundance of flowers – eye-catching and colourful plants that make a bold impact. This isn't *Alchemilla*. Instead, the lady's mantle is a quiet, understated and extremely hard-working herbaceous perennial that should not be overlooked.

ALCHEMILLA MOLLIS
LADY'S MANTLE
▼

NEED TO KNOW

—

SIZE
UP TO 50cm (20in)
TALL AND 50cm
(20in) WIDE

—

LIGHT
FULL SUN TO
DAPPLED SHADE

—

SOIL TYPE
CLAY, SAND, CHALK
OR LOAM

—

MOISTURE
MOIST BUT
WELL DRAINED

—

VARIETIES
A. mollis, lady's mantle;
A. erythropoda, dwarf
lady's mantle; *A. alpina*,
alpine lady's mantle;
A. conjuncta, silver
lady's mantle

WHY GROW IT

Lady's mantle comes into its own just after it has rained, as the droplets of water bead on the foliage and create the most mesmerising effect. Indeed, the origin of the name *Alchemilla* suggests the plant's use in the ancient art of alchemy, where the dew that collected on the leaves was used for medicinal purposes. Its foamy mist of butter-yellow flowers splays from the finely serrated foliage, both of which happen to be great used in cut flower arrangements.

WHERE TO PUT IT

A front-of-border plant that helps to break down and soften path edges, use lady's mantle in almost any situation – it is immensely versatile. Working as a contrasting background for surrounding planting, it really is one of the best foliage plants you can use in the garden. Due to its low-growing nature, it also lends itself well to growing in pots and containers, and it sits very comfortably in a typical cottage-style garden.

HOW TO LOOK AFTER IT

Make sure it doesn't dry out during the summer months – although it does love full sun, it also thrives on moisture. That aside, it is a reliable plant that is relatively maintenance-free. Indeed, sometimes it can grow too well, and may begin to spread across the garden into unwanted areas. Should this happen, dig up some clumps and share them with a friend. After all, a weed is only a plant in the wrong place.

DO

Use in flower arrangements – the foliage helps to break up strong colours

Cut back faded flowers and tired foliage – both will grow back

Feed throughout the year with an organic seaweed-based fertiliser

DON'T

Plant in full shade – it will survive, but it needs sunlight to flower and flourish

Plant among larger growing plants, as it will be smothered

Let it dry out completely – it is not completely drought-tolerant

01

01. *ALCHEMILLA ERYTHROPODA*
    DWARF LADY'S MANTLE
    A smaller-growing *Alchemilla* that
    grows well in cracks and crevices,
    dwarf lady's mantle is very well
    behaved, forming compact mounds
    of delicate soft-green foliage.

02. *ALCHEMILLA ALPINA*
    ALPINE LADY'S MANTLE
    Very low-growing, almost hugging
    the floor, Alpine lady's mantle has
    slightly glossier foliage and tiny
    creamy yellow flowers, perfect for
    a rockery garden.

03. *ALCHEMILLA CONJUNCTA*
    SILVER LADY'S MANTLE
    A delicate and delightfully small
    Alchemilla that has shiny foliage,
    with a silvery tint to the leaves,
    silver lady's mantle is clump-
    forming and easy to grow.

THRIFT AND OTHER ALPINE PLANTS

Every garden, no matter how big or small, has cracks and crevices where it can be difficult to know what will grow. These unique planting pockets may often be overlooked, and yet they can be a prized addition to the garden, offering space in which a whole range of alpine plants can establish and grow. Alpine plants naturally originate from mountainous regions, where the ground is rocky, and they have adapted to grow in the tightest of spaces. Thrift is one plant that flourishes in these tough conditions.

ARMERIA MARITIMA 'SPLENDENS' THRIFT
▼

NEED TO KNOW

—

SIZE
15CM (6IN)

—

LIGHT
FULL SUN

—

SOIL TYPE
SAND, CLAY, CHALK
OR LOAM

—

MOISTURE
WELL DRAINED

—

VARIETIES
A. maritima
'Splendens', thrift;
Erigeron karvinskianus,
Mexican fleabane;
Campanula poscharskyana,
trailing bellflower;
Aubrieta 'Red Cascade'

WHY GROW IT

Thrift is as easy to grow as they come, and yet for such minimal effort, you will be rewarded with dozens of bright, zingy pink flowers all spring, throughout summer and into the autumn. The bees adore its chive-like flowers, and it doesn't grow very big at all, so it makes an ideal ground cover plant. If you are looking for a plant to try and grow for the very first time, then this is it.

WHERE TO PUT IT

Thrift can be found growing naturally around the coastline and especially on exposed cliffs. It readily self-seeds in cracks and crevices, and these exposed sites give an indication of the sort of conditions it prefers. It loves full sun, good drainage and plenty of room to send down its roots. When replicating this in your own garden, try and find the sunniest spot possible, and mix thrift with other alpine plants for the ultimate low-maintenance garden.

HOW TO LOOK AFTER IT

Thrift is simplicity itself – just leave it to do its own thing. It is much happier when left to grow than when nurtured and fed. It doesn't succumb to pests or diseases and can withstand any UK winter (so long as it isn't too wet).

DO

Plant thrift into cracks and crevices

Use a very free-draining, sandy compost mixture if growing in pots

Use it to attract bees and butterflies – it is perfect for pollinators

DON'T

Worry about giving these plants too much love or attention – they almost thrive on neglect

Plant in shade – it needs as much sunlight as possible

Prune it – just clip off the spent flowers to keep it tidy

THREE TO TRY

01

01. *ERIGERON KARVINSKIANUS* MEXICAN FLEABANE

Mexican fleabane is an amazing perennial that produces hundreds of tiny daisy-like flowers through the spring and summer, drifting and dancing through walling and paving. Grow in full sun with good drainage.

02. *CAMPANULA POSCHARSKYANA* TRAILING BELLFLOWER

The trailing bellflower lives up to its name, producing masses of light-purple bell-like flowers throughout the summer months. These delicate little star-shaped flowers can be very vigorous once they get going.

03. *AUBRIETA* 'RED CASCADE'

Another fabulous ground cover, trailing and spreading plant that can happily establish itself within walls or paving. In late spring it produces an abundance of bright red flowers that adore full sun.

02

03

FERN

Ferns are an amazing group of plants that provide us with lush greenery in the darkest and dampest of corners, where most other plants would curl up their leaves and refuse to grow. Outside of gardens, ferns can be found growing in the most random of places, from cracks in walling to deep, dark woodlands; under bridges and out of drains.

ASPLENIUM
SCOLOPENDRIUM
HART'S TONGUE FERN
▶

NEED TO KNOW
—

SIZE
NORMALLY AROUND
30CM (12IN)
—

LIGHT
FULL TO
PARTIAL SHADE
—

SOIL TYPE
SAND, CLAY, CHALK
OR LOAM
—

MOISTURE
MOIST BUT
WELL DRAINED
—

WHY GROW IT
Asplenium has long, leathery, textured foliage that is a vivid dark green. The fronds unfurl and reach out like a dog stretching after a long sleep. They are simple, structural and will give your garden interest all year round.

WHERE TO PUT IT
Ferns are tolerant of most types of shade, including dry shade, making them ideal for planting under trees or large shrubs. Place them in a woodland setting, or even just next to a north-facing wall, where they can be protected from direct sunlight.

HOW TO LOOK AFTER IT
Cut back the faded fronds to allow lush new foliage to push through. After several years, give the fern quite a harsh cut back to ground level; it will respond with vigour and a new lease of life. Make sure the fern doesn't dry out. Despite being tolerant of dry shade, it needs plenty of water to thrive, especially in the first growing year.

DO

Plant it in that shady spot in the garden where nothing else will grow

Mulch the ground around the plant with compost or bark to help retain moisture

Grow it in pots – that way you can move the plant around the garden to help find the best spot for it

DON'T

Plant it out in full sun – the foliage will become scorched and yellow

Let it dry out, especially in the first growing season

Worry about trying to propagate it – this can be complicated and they often propagate themselves anyway

OTHERS TO TRY

—

DRYOPTERIS ERYTHROSORA
'BRILLIANCE'
COPPER SHIELD FERN
Huge, bright yellow flowers
up to 75cm (30in) high.

—

ATHYRIUM FILIX-FEMINA
LADY FERN
Growing to around 80cm (32in)
tall, its finely cut soft-green foliage
works to soften planting and add a
splash of calm.

—

POLYSTICHUM SETIFERUM
SOFT SHIELD FERN
Growing to around 1.2m (4ft)
tall, it is sure to add drama to
woodland planting. Cut back to
ground level in spring, and watch
the new leaves unfurl.

WALLFLOWER

A group of plants typically associated with your grandparents' cutting garden, wallflowers are commonly overlooked as block-coloured bedding plants lacking in style. But don't write them all off. In fact, there are a group of perennial wallflowers that not only dispel these stigmas but are actually one of the most reliable and hard-working plants you could ask for in the garden. With blooms that don't quite understand the conventional flowering seasons, they tend to flower throughout most of the year.

ERYSIMUM
'BOWLES'S MAUVE'
WALLFLOWER
▼

SIZE
UP TO 75CM
(30IN) TALL
—

LIGHT
FULL SUN
—

SOIL TYPE
SAND, CHALK
OR LOAM
—

MOISTURE
WELL DRAINED
—

VARIETIES
E. 'Bowles's Mauve';
E. 'Apricot Twist';
E. 'Red Jep';
E. 'Winter Orchid'

WHY GROW IT

Producing flowers from mid-spring right the way through to the autumn, the wallflower is a plant that just doesn't know when to give up. Its endurance is more than impressive, and just one of the reasons it was a close contender for the RHS Plant of the Centenary award. The foliage is a grey-green colour and creates the perfect foil for the flowers to stand out.

WHERE TO PUT IT

Find the sunniest spot in the garden, preferably in front of a south-facing wall (hence the name), where it can bask in the heat and flower away. Although it does exceptionally well when planted in the ground in a free-draining soil, it will also do just as well in containers.

HOW TO LOOK AFTER IT

To help keep the wallflower on its seemingly never-ending flowering mission, keep cutting back the flowers that have finished to free up energy and space for more to come through. The plants will become woody with age and can begin to rock around in the wind; to counter this, plant them slightly deeper than normal. You should feed wallflowers every few months to help maintain their energy levels throughout the year.

DO

Deadhead regularly to ensure it keeps flowering throughout the summer – it can be a bit fiddly in this case but it is worth the effort

Plant alongside pure white tulips for a classy spring container

Use in drought-tolerant planting combinations

DON'T

Grow in clay – this can cause the soil to become waterlogged in the winter months

Worry if the plant dies after a few years – although these are technically perennials, they can sometimes be short-lived

Plant in shade – they need full sun to thrive

THREE TO TRY

01

02

01. *ERYSIMUM* 'APRICOT TWIST'
If you love a zing of orange, *Erysimum* 'Apricot Twist' is the variety for you. Bright and cheerful orange flowers are produced all spring and into early summer.

02. *ERYSIMUM* 'RED JEP'
A spectacularly scented brother of *Erysimum* 'Bowles's Mauve', again, flowering for most of the year, the flowers of 'Red Jep' are an eye-catching crimson colour, ideal for making a bold statement.

03. *ERYSIMUM* 'WINTER ORCHID'
It's a slightly more garish cocktail of pink and orange that can divide opinion, but if you're looking for something slightly different that smells great and puts on a spectacular show, you should definitely consider this *Erysimum*.

03

EUPHORBIA

SPURGE

———

The _Euphorbiaceae_ family – aka spurges – is a huge group of plants that features thousands of different species. Although most are succulents, the herbaceous varieties offer an exciting array of textural foliage and vibrant blue, green and golden colours. One of the most popular is _E. characias_ subsp. _wulfenii_, or Mediterranean spurge.

EUPHORBIA CHARACIAS
SUBSP. _WULFENII_
MEDITERRANEAN
SPURGE
▼

SIZE
UP TO 1.5M
(5FT) HIGH

—

LIGHT
FULL OR PARTIAL SUN

—

SOIL TYPE
SAND, LOAM, CHALK

—

MOISTURE
WELL DRAINED

—

VARIETIES
E. characias subsp. *wulfenii*,
Mediterranean spurge;
E. tirucalli 'Firecracker';
E. mellifera; E. amygdaloides
var. *robbiae*, wood spurge

WHY GROW IT

These plants are drought resistant, meaning they require virtually no watering in the summer, and are practically pest and disease free. They provide whorls of attractive, blue-green evergreen foliage all year round on individual stems. The flowers are their crowning glory, when in spring the tips produce huge clusters of acid-lime flower bracts held aloft on stiff stems.

WHERE TO PUT IT

Many euphorbias, such as *E. characias* subsp. *wulfenii*, are unfussy about soil conditions and tend to thrive in any soil as long as it is well drained. It should be grown outside in either full or partial sun. Avoid completely shady situations and places where it may be exposed to wind. These plants look their best when grown in an herbaceous border, usually in the middle with smaller plants grown in front. Their evergreen foliage provides a wonderful contrast and foil to neighbouring flowers for most of the year, and their almost neon yellow flowering stems create a vivid splash of colour in spring.

HOW TO LOOK AFTER IT

Euphorbias are fairly low maintenance – you just need to cut back the flower stems to near ground level once the flowers have gone over. A word of warning though: do be careful not to get the milky white sap on your skin, and definitely not in your eyes or mouth, as it is a toxic irritant.

DO

Wear gloves when handling them and wash your hands immediately if you do come into contact with the sap

Propagate by dividing the plant in early spring, prior to flowering

Dip cut flower stems in warm water before arranging to prevent the sap leaking out

DON'T

Eat it – the sap is toxic

Overfeed or mollycoddle it – it is happy being left to do its own thing

Trim it like a bush. Cut back individual stems to the ground if necessary

01

02

01. *EUPHORBIA TIRUCALLI*
    'FIRECRACKER'
    A 45cm (18in) high euphorbia with
    bright orange–red flowers.

02. *EUPHORBIA MELLIFERA*
    A medium-sized evergreen shrub
    with honey smelling flowers.

03. *EUPHORBIA AMYGDALOIDES*
    VAR. *ROBBIAE*
    A small ground cover plant with
    wonderful acid yellow spring colour.

03

SALVIA

The *Salvia* genus is a big one, with dozens of delightful varieties to choose from. Some of the most spectacular varieties, such as *Salvia nemorosa* 'Caradonna', feature spires of majestic purple flowers rising over a compact mound of foliage. The plant's combination of decorum and versatility makes it a great addition to any garden.

SALVIA NEMOROSA 'CARADONNA' BALKAN CLARY
▼

SIZE
UP TO 50cm (20in) TALL

LIGHT
PREFERS FULL SUN
BUT WILL TOLERATE
PARTIAL SHADE

SOIL TYPE
SAND, LOAM
OR CHALK

MOISTURE
MOIST BUT
WELL DRAINED

VARIETIES
S. nemorosa 'Caradonna',
Balkan clary;
S. 'Nachtvlinder';
S. guaranitica
'Black and Blue';
S. × sylvestris 'Mainacht'

WHY GROW IT

I am a big fan of plants that just 'get on with it', and that's why I always grow *Salvia*. It is a staple plant for most gardeners and garden designers alike, due to its ability to flower from May right the way through to the first frosts. Even then, it continues to persevere, as the skeletal flower stems catch the morning dew and hard frosts.

WHERE TO PUT IT

Salvias adore full sun. They will tolerate dappled shade, but the sunnier it is, the better they will grow. Due to the plant's compact nature, it also lends itself well to being grown in a pot or container, so it will work even if you don't have much space at all. *Salvia* is ideal in a mixed border, wildlife garden, cottage garden or dry garden – anywhere really!

HOW TO LOOK AFTER IT

The key to success with this plant is to ensure it doesn't sit too wet throughout the winter months. Though it is hardy, it doesn't like the wet. Because of this, you should avoid growing it in clay soils where possible. In February cut the plant back to ground level, mulch with some good old organic matter and watch it spring back to life.

DO

Cut it back once it has finished flowering and it will reward you with a succession of flowers for the rest of the year

Use the plant to attract wildlife into the garden – bees and butterflies can't get enough of it

Use it as a cut flower – the flowering spires make a great addition to bouquets

DON'T

Plant in heavy shade – it won't flower and will struggle to survive

Grow it in clay – it needs a light, free-draining soil to perform at its best

Cut back the flowers in the winter – leave them on the plant and they will add architecture to the winter garden

01

02

03

01. SALVIA 'NACHTVLINDER'
'Nachtvlinder' looks great planted into containers and will flower for months on end, producing delicate, deep-purple blooms. It looks fantastic planted with Mexican feather grass (see page 52).

02. SALVIA GUARANITICA 'BLACK AND BLUE'
A dark *Salvia* that really stands out, adding depth to borders. Flowering all through summer and autumn, and growing to 2m (6.5ft) tall, it is a must-have for any large border.

03. SALVIA × SYLVESTRIS 'MAINACHT'
This is similar to 'Caradonna', but prefers moister ground, so if you have a slightly damper garden, this would be a better option. Spires of majestic purple grow to around 75cm (30in) tall.

BURNET

Sanguisorba are some of my all-time favourite plants: beautiful, versatile and foolproof – what's not to love? Having first grown them as a child, I remember being mesmerised by the tight clusters of flowers that bobble around in the wind, earning them their nickname of 'bobble heads'. Some varieties are particularly easy to grow, and feature long stems that allow the flower clusters to waft gently in the breeze.

SANGUISORBA
OFFICINALIS
'RED THUNDER'
GREAT BURNET
▼

SIZE

BETWEEN 1M (3FT)

AND 1.5M (5FT) TALL

—

LIGHT

FULL SUN TO

PARTIAL SHADE

—

SOIL TYPE

SAND, CLAY, CHALK

OR LOAM

—

MOISTURE

MOIST BUT

WELL DRAINED

—

VARIETIES

S. officinalis
'Red Thunder', great
burnet; *S. canadensis*,
Canadian burnet;
S. hakusanensis 'Lilac
Squirrel'; *S. officinalis*
'Chocolate Tip'

WHY GROW IT

The prairie nature of this perennial makes it great for natural planting, as you can leave the plants to self-sow, spread and generally get on with it. Another thing I encourage people to look for when choosing plants is how the plants die (yes, really). If you can grow plants that maintain elegance and decorum after they finish flowering, then you can extend the season of interest throughout the winter for free.

WHERE TO PUT IT

For maximum impact, plant burnet among grasses and other tall, airy perennials to create a highly textured border. The plant's unfussy nature makes it great to grow in a whole range of locations, but it should ideally be positioned in full sun or dappled shade, with good, free-draining soil.

HOW TO LOOK AFTER IT

Once you've found the right location, the rest is easy! Cut back the dead growth in late winter. You don't need to be too precious about this — hedge shears will do the job a lot quicker and easier than anything else. The new growth will be produced from late March onwards. As the plant starts to grow, provide it with some support to stop it flopping over in heavy rain.

DO

Plant it alongside grasses —
the combination creates an
airy, natural effect

Stake the plants as they
grow to prevent them from
flopping in heavy rain

Cut back in May to create stronger
plants and squat flower stems

DON'T

Let it dry out too much, as it can
become susceptible to mildew (a white
powder on the surface of the foliage)

Plant in full shade — it needs the
sunlight to perform best

Cut it back until February, once its
bobble heads have had a chance
to catch the winter frosts

SANGUISORBA
THREE TO TRY

01

02

01. SANGUISORBA CANADENSIS
CANADIAN BURNET
An upright and tall-growing
Sanguisorba originating from North
America, Canadian burnet is ideal
for large gardens. It produces white
flower spikes late into the summer
and autumn.

02. SANGUISORBA HAKUSANENSIS
'LILAC SQUIRREL'
For lovers of something a little
different, 'Lilac Squirrel' grows to
around 1m (3ft) tall and has fluffy,
lilac-purple flowers that resemble
a squirrel's tail.

03. SANGUISORBA OFFICINALIS
'CHOCOLATE TIP'
This variety has chocolate-coloured
flowers. Only growing to around
80cm (32in) tall, it's happier towards
the front of a border.

03

STIPA (NEEDLE GRASS)

Grasses may not have the flower power of many of the other plants in this book, but they do play an important role in the garden, providing structure, architecture and texture to planting that may otherwise become too overpowering. By introducing grasses, you create a foil against which the flowering plants can shine. A type of needle grass would be the ideal plant for this.

STIPA TENUISSIMA
MEXICAN FEATHER
GRASS
▼

SIZE
UP TO 60cm (24in) TALL

LIGHT
FULL SUN

SOIL TYPE
SAND, CLAY, CHALK
OR LOAM

MOISTURE
WELL DRAINED

VARIETIES
S. tenuissima,
mexican feather grass;
Anemanthele lessoniana,
pheasant's tail grass;
Sesleria caerulea,
blue moor-grass;
Deschampsia cespitosa,
tufted hair grass

WHY GROW IT

The delicate, wispy seed heads wave in the breeze and really do add an extra layer of interest. Yet despite this soft and flimsy appearance, indeterminate stipa is remarkably hardy. Its translucent seed heads light up in the evening sun, highlighting their golden locks, which mature gracefully as the year goes on.

WHERE TO PUT IT

Planted in full sun, you can't go wrong. With this in mind, gravel and dry gardens make the ideal spot for needle grass. However, it will also fit in very happily in a cottage-style garden, wildlife garden, container garden or even just at path edges to soften and break up harsh lines.

HOW TO LOOK AFTER IT

The common mistake people make with this plant is chopping it back too early. Save your energy and leave it well alone over the winter months. Come the spring, gently rake out the dead foliage using your fingers and leave the remaining foliage behind. A quick tidy-up is all the plant requires, although should you cut the grass right back, it will grow.

DO

Plant with annuals in containers
for a light and airy effect

Grow in full sun – it can
tolerate dry weather

Grow it en masse where possible –
this isn't easy in a small garden, but if
you've got the space, go for it

DON'T

Cut it right back in the autumn –
instead, wait until spring then rake
out any dead growth with your fingers

Let it sit in wet soil over the winter
months – this could cause it to rot

Allow it to spread into unwanted
areas – should this happen, dig them
out and gift the spares to a friend

01

02

01. *ANEMANTHELE LESSONIANA*
PHEASANT'S TAIL GRASS
Pheasant's tail grass is a fantastic
plant that gives you year-round
interest. It has an amazingly colourful
foliage that intensifies during winter,
and it produces impressive seed
heads during the summer months.

02. *SESLERIA CAERULEA*
BLUE MOOR-GRASS
These low-growing clumps of
muted blue-green leaves are ideal
for sun-parched areas of the garden.
The grass's foliage is its major
attraction but it does also produce
small cream-coloured seed heads.

03. *DESCHAMPSIA CESPITOSA*
TUFTED HAIR GRASS
An earlier-flowering grass that
can often be found on display at
the RHS Chelsea Flower Show.
It is able to tie planting together
and put on a show itself, growing
up to 1m (3ft) tall.

03

VERBENA

Verbena is a family of plants loved as much by the bees and butterflies as it is by us gardeners. Despite its gracious and airy appearance, *Verbena* is an incredibly tough and resilient plant that will withstand the hottest of summers, making it one of my top ten indestructible perennials.

VERBENA BONARIENSIS
ARGENTINIAN
VERVAIN
▼

SIZE
UP TO 2m
(6.5ft) TALL
—

LIGHT
FULL SUN
—

SOIL TYPE
CLAY, SAND, CHALK
OR LOAM
—

MOISTURE
FREE DRAINING
—

VARIETIES
V. bonariensis,
Argentinian vervain;
V. bonariensis 'Lollipop';
V. rigida, hardy garden
verbena; *V. macdougalii*
'Lavender Spires'

WHY GROW IT

Verbena is a great option for bringing wildlife, structure, colour and interest into the garden. Flowering from the end of June through to the first frosts, it knows how to perform. Even when it's finished flowering, the old flower heads mature, looking slightly silvery in the morning light, and will provide architecture throughout the winter months. *Verbena* also lends itself well to being used as a cut flower, thanks to its very rigid, upright stems. The flowers, of which there can be thousands, are formed in tightly packed little clusters the size of a two-pound coin, and create a perfect landing spot for incoming bees.

WHERE TO PUT IT

Verbena adores a south-facing, sunny spot with good drainage. It isn't fussy about soil type just so long as it doesn't sit wet for too long. Originating from South America, it really does enjoy the heat. With this in mind, gravel gardens offer a great planting location. If you don't have a gravel garden (don't worry, I don't either), then a largish pot with a very light, free-draining compost will do perfectly.

HOW TO LOOK AFTER IT

A master in self-sufficiency, *Verbena* really does just get on with life. Aside from watering when the plants are new and need to become established, and perhaps when the weather gets very hot (July to August), they do just look after themselves. Sit back and enjoy the hundreds of pincushion purple flowers all summer long. Cut it back in late winter.

DO

Plant it at the back of a border so it doesn't shade out other plants

Stake clumps if they begin to flop when growing – for a natural look, use coppiced birch stems

Plant it in a wildlife garden – the bees absolutely adore its abundance of flowers

DON'T

Cut it back once it's finished flowering – the plants will naturally self-seed and give you free flowers for the following year

Plant it in the shade – *Verbena* needs full sun to thrive

Forget to water it – although it is almost indestructible, it will need some water during very hot spells

THREE TO TRY

01

01. *VERBENA BONARIENSIS*
    'LOLLIPOP'
    'Lollipop' is a smaller, more compact
    Verbena – ideal if you have less
    space and are looking to grow it
    in a pot or container.

02. *VERBENA RIGIDA*
    HARDY GARDEN VERBENA
    A small *Verbena* ideal for container
    growing, *V. rigida* produces stunning
    deep-purple flowers on rigid stems
    for months on end. One of
    my favourites!

03. *VERBENA MACDOUGALII*
    'LAVENDER SPIRES'
    As the name suggests, lavender-
    coloured flowers are produced from
    July to October. The plants grow up
    to 2m (6.5ft) tall, with very erect
    flower spikes.

02

03

5

SHRUBS

THAT YOU
CAN'T KILL

WINTER DOGWOOD

CORNUS

62

FUCHSIA

FUCHSIA

66

HYDRANGEA

HYDRANGEA

70

CHEESEWOOD

PITTOSPORUM

74

GUELDER-ROSE

VIBURNUM OPULUS

78

WINTER DOGWOOD

Gardens shouldn't look good just in the summer months, but all year round. It's not difficult to add structure and interest to the garden during the winter months, when just a smattering of colour can go a long way to cheering up a cold, damp day. Dogwoods are a diverse family: ranging from structural plants providing interest in winter to fabulous spring-flowering dogwoods, there really is one for every style of garden.

CORNUS ALBA
'SIBIRICA'
SIBERIAN DOGWOOD
▼

SIZE
UP TO 2.5M (8FT) TALL
—

LIGHT
FULL SUN OR
PARTIAL SHADE
—

SOIL TYPE
SAND, CLAY OR LOAM
—

MOISTURE
MOIST BUT
WELL DRAINED
—

VARIETIES
C. alba 'Sibirica',
siberian dogwood;
C. sanguinea 'Midwinter Fire';
C. kousa 'China Girl';
C. controversa 'Variegata'

WHY GROW IT

Dogwoods grow superbly in a multitude of positions and suit all kinds of gardens. From stunning spring flowers through to an incredible winter structure, there is a *Cornus* for every space. The winter dogwoods produce an exceptional display of vibrant colour throughout the coldest months, making it an uplifting plant that is sure to impress. Its versatility makes it a firm favourite among gardeners.

WHERE TO PUT IT

Dogwood will grow just about anywhere; it is happy in most types of soil and doesn't mind a bit of shade.

HOW TO LOOK AFTER IT

This is truly one of the easiest shrubs to grow. For the very best and most vivid winter displays, the key is to cut the old stems back to ground level in late winter. Throughout the spring and summer, the shrub will then produce fresh, bright shoots for the following winter.

DO

Leave the stems over winter and cut back to ground level in March

Use the cut stems in flower arrangements

Mix with other richly coloured winter dogwoods for a fiery winter display

DON'T

Cut back the stems before the winter – that's why you're growing it, after all

Grow in shade – for the best winter colour, grow in full sun

Let it dry out during hot summers, as this can stress the plant and scorch the foliage

THREE TO TRY

01

01. *CORNUS SANGUINEA* 'MIDWINTER FIRE'
Similar in stature to 'Sibirica', but with much more intensely coloured stems that, from a distance, appear to be ablaze. When planted en masse, they really are something to behold.

02. *CORNUS KOUSA* 'CHINA GIRL'
This is a spring-flowering dogwood that can grow up to 7m (23ft) tall, so it is like a small tree. In most gardens, however, it is grown as a large shrub.

03. *CORNUS CONTROVERSA* 'VARIEGATA'
This dogwood is grown for its superb variegated foliage that creates a tiered effect, giving the plant its nickname of the wedding cake tree. It is perfect if you have a slightly larger garden in which it can spread out and show off.

02

03

FUCHSIA

There is so much to love about the *Fuchsia*, the summer-flowering shrub that quietly gets on with things. This plant puts on a show that would rival any perennial, but without the looking after. It's an honest grafter that can add colour to any garden throughout the summer, and there's an option for every size of garden; many cultivars grow well in hanging baskets but lots of fuchsias will die over winter if they are not protected.

FUCHSIA
'HAWKSHEAD'
FUCHSIA
▼

—

SIZE
UP TO 1 M (3 FT) TALL
BY 50 CM (20 IN) WIDE

—

LIGHT
FULL SUN OR PARTIAL
SHADE

—

SOIL TYPE
SAND, CLAY, CHALK
OR LOAM

—

MOISTURE
MOIST BUT WELL
DRAINED

—

VARIETIES
F. 'Hawkshead';
F. 'Mrs Popple';
F. 'Riccartonii'
F. 'Annabel'

WHY GROW IT

Fuchsias are a staple plant of any cottage garden and are a fond favourite for most gardeners thanks to their prolific flowering and impressive endurance. Bell-like flowers are produced from tubular buds from spring all the way through to early autumn.

WHERE TO PUT IT

Fuchsias grow best in fertile soil that gets sun for most of the day. Keeping it sheltered during the colder months is key, so if you are growing it in a container, it's best to move it to a less exposed spot in winter. Varieties such as 'Hawkshead'; lend themselves well to being grown in a cottage-style garden or shrub border. Their loose growth habit softens surrounding planting and, if planted densely, it can even make a low, informal hedge.

HOW TO LOOK AFTER IT

When planting out, bury the plant slightly deeper than it was in its original pot. This helps to protect the roots from cold weather. Mulching during the winter can also provide extra protection. During the flowering season, feed and water regularly to keep the display going as long as possible. Prune in early spring, cutting branches back to the main framework of the plant.

DO

Pinch out the tips as they are growing to encourage the plants to bush out

Prune back to near ground level in early spring for a great summer display

Feed regularly to encourage continual flowering

DON'T

Grow in an exposed site where it can become vulnerable to winter winds

Prune too early – leave it until the end of winter or early spring before cutting back

Allow the plant to dry out during the summer months

THREE TO TRY

01

01. *FUCHSIA* 'MRS POPPLE'
'Mrs Popple' is a reliable and easy-to-grow *Fuchsia* that's a great option for a shadier garden. Red petals shelter a frilly purple centre.

02. *FUCHSIA* 'RICCARTONII'
With similar flowers to 'Mrs Popple' (only more slender) produced in profusion, this is a much bigger plant that works well as a large shrub and will add bulk to the garden.

03. *FUCHSIA* 'ANNABEL'
This cultivar produces double white flowers tinged with sublime pink. It's a much smaller-growing *Fuchsia* that will grow brilliantly in containers.

02

03

HYDRANGEA

Hydrangeas are one of my favourite shrubs to grow, thanks to their bold and impressive flower heads that add theatre and drama to the garden. Despite looking flamboyant and blowsy, they are actually very easy to grow and tolerant of most conditions, and they will perform reliably year upon year.

HYDRANGEA PANICULATA
'LIMELIGHT'
PANICULATE HYDRANGEA
▼

SIZE
UP TO 2.5M (8FT) HIGH
AND 1.5M (5FT) WIDE
—

LIGHT
FULL SUN OR
PARTIAL SHADE
—

SOIL TYPE
SAND, CLAY OR LOAM
—

MOISTURE
MOIST BUT
WELL DRAINED
—

VARIETIES
H. paniculata 'Limelight',
paniculate hydrangea;
H. anomala subsp.
petiolaris, climbing
hydrangea; *H. arborescens*
'Annabelle'; *H. macrophylla*
'Kardinal Violet'

WHY GROW IT
Large cones of flowers stand tall like giant ice cream cones. The blooms hold well throughout the winter months, continuing to provide structure right into spring before the shrub is pruned back.

WHERE TO PUT IT
Find a position that gets sun for most of the day but offers some shelter. Dappled shade is ideal and helps to keep the plant cool during the heat of the summer. The *Hydrangea* works well integrated into a mixed shrub border, as an informal hedge or even just as an impressive focal point in a container. It will look at home in a whole range of settings, from traditional cottage gardens to contemporary courtyards.

HOW TO LOOK AFTER IT
The clue to growing really good hydrangeas is in the name: *hydor* is Greek for water. Make sure they don't dry out, especially during the summer months. They are big plants that can become very thirsty, and keeping them constantly hydrated is the key to impressive blooms. Prune back to the old wood in late winter, cutting back the previous year's growth to two buds from the main framework.

DO

Use as large cut flowers – six stems in a vase is plenty to create a long-lasting indoor display

Grow in a fertile soil that has plenty of moisture

Plant in large containers as a specimen plant (or focal point) – standalone plants can make a simple but effective display

DON'T

Prune back until late winter – this allows you to enjoy the structural seed heads throughout the colder months

Plant in full shade – it requires some sunlight to thrive

Allow the plant to dry out – keep it constantly moist, especially during summer

HYDRANGEA

THREE TO TRY

01

02

01. *HYDRANGEA ANOMALA*
   SUBSP. PETIOLARIS
   CLIMBING HYDRANGEA
   A climbing *Hydrangea* that has large
   white lacecap flowers throughout
   summer. It has self-climbing abilities,
   making it ideal to grow up a large,
   prominent tree, even in full shade.

02. *HYDRANGEA ARBORESCENS*
   'ANNABELLE'
   One of my all-time favourite
   hydrangeas thanks to its simple,
   large and creamy white flower
   heads, which can grow to football
   size. Plant several in a row against
   a wall for maximum impact.

03. *HYDRANGEA MACROPHYLLA*
   'KARDINAL VIOLET'
   These hydrangeas are much more
   compact shrubs with dozens of
   lacecap flowers that vary in colour
   depending on the pH of the soil.

03

CHEESEWOOD

——

Pittosporum is a hard-working, easy-to-grow and reliable shrub that provides year-round structure to the garden. A superb alternative to using box (*Buxus sempervirens*), cheesewood can be tightly clipped to give that same topiary-style appearance, used as low hedging or just as a focal piece. The lush mounds are very versatile, lending themselves to a whole range of garden situations.

PITTOSPORUM TENUIFOLIUM 'TOM THUMB'
▼

—

SIZE
UP TO 1M (3FT) TALL
AND 1M (3FT) IN SPREAD

—

LIGHT
FULL SUN OR
PARTIAL SHADE

—

SOIL TYPE
SAND, CHALK
OR LOAM

—

MOISTURE
MOIST BUT
WELL DRAINED

—

VARIETIES
P. tenuifolium 'Tom Thumb';
P. tenuifolium 'Golf Ball';
P. tobira 'Nanum', dwarf
Japanese mock orange;
P. tenuifolium 'Silver Queen'

WHY GROW IT

Cheesewood is a brilliant, dense, low-growing and dependable shrub with small, dense, waxy foliage. Its new growth is a fresh green in spring and fades to a deep purple that continues to look great all year. Cheesewood provides structure, texture and architecture to planting, but without the worry of continual maintenance.

WHERE TO PUT IT

Pittosporum love a sunny and free-draining site, but avoid planting them anywhere too open; they don't like cold winds and can sometimes be vulnerable to frosts. Low-growing varieties lend themselves well to pots and containers, and it can easily be grown in a large border where they can be allowed to grow slightly bigger. Use them to punctuate flowerbeds.

HOW TO LOOK AFTER IT

Very easy to look after and grow, *Pittosporum's* slow-growing nature means it requires next to no maintenance, just very infrequent clipping if you wish to keep the foliage dense and compact. Spread a thick layer of mulch around the base of the shrub during the winter months to help protect its roots from frost.

DO

Use it as a great alternative
to box hedges

Plant in clusters and allow the
domes to merge into each other,
creating a cloud-like effect

Use the foliage to break up
large areas of colour and add
structure to the garden

DON'T

Grow in an exposed site where
it can become susceptible to
cold winds or frost damage

Cut it back too hard – lightly prune
in early spring to maintain its shape

Grow in shade – it loves full sun

THREE TO TRY

01

01. **PITTOSPORUM TENUIFOLIUM**
'GOLF BALL'
A compact cultivar that is a
fresh lime-green colour. 'Golf Ball'
grows into small domes that will
tie planting together or look great
alone in containers.

02. **PITTOSPORUM TOBIRA 'NANUM'**
DWARF JAPANESE
MOCK ORANGE
'Nanum' is a fleshier, low-growing
Pittosporum that creates a compact
mound similar to that of a dumpling.
The larger, glossy foliage has a
tropical appearance.

03. **PITTOSPORUM TENUIFOLIUM**
'SILVER QUEEN'
'Silver Queen' is a much larger-
growing *Pittosporum*, making
it ideal for screening or hedging.
The light-green leaves are edged
with white, giving them a light and
unobtrusive appearance.

02

03

GUELDER-ROSE

Viburnum will happily grow just about anywhere. And yet despite its versatile, indestructible nature, it produces clusters of delicate flowers throughout the spring months.

VIBURNUM OPULUS
'ROSEUM'
SNOWBALL TREE
▼

SIZE

UP TO 4M (13FT) TALL

—

LIGHT

FULL SUN, PARTIAL
SHADE OR EVEN
FULL SHADE

—

SOIL TYPE

SAND, CLAY, CHALK
OR LOAM

—

MOISTURE

MOIST BUT
WELL DRAINED

—

VARIETIES

V. opulus 'Roseum',
snowball tree; *V. tinus*, syn.
laurustinus; *V. plicatum*
'Mariesii', Japanese
snowball; *V. burkwoodii*,
Burkwood viburnum

WHY GROW IT

When considering plants for the garden it's important to think about not only flower and colour, but also height and structure. *Viburnum* is a plant that can provide both.

WHERE TO PUT IT

You can plant *Viburnum* just about anywhere that has room for it to grow and mature; this is a space-filler that can be used as an informal hedge or a focal point at the back of a border. It will grow in just about any soil type, and in any position in the garden.

HOW TO LOOK AFTER IT

Viburnum is as easy to look after as they come, but keep an eye out for viburnum beetle, a small beetle that can eat holes in the foliage, causing the plant to become unsightly. The adults are small and grey, but the larvae – who do most of the damage – are a creamy yellow colour. Prune off any infected branches and destroy them. Although an infestation can look disastrous, it doesn't normally kill the plant.

DO

Use it in a low-maintenance garden that requires structure and height

Mulch generously around the base of the shrub to prevent it from drying out

Use as a cut flower – combine it with spring flowers for a stunning display

DON'T

Be afraid to cut it back hard if it becomes too big – it is very tolerant of hard pruning

Grow in a small garden – it needs space to establish and mature

Give it too much time or attention – it thrives on neglect

THREE TO TRY

01

02

03

01. VIBURNUM TINUS
LAURUSTINUS
Glossy evergreen leaves make this a great all-round shrub that will prove virtually unkillable. With the added benefit of white flower clusters throughout winter and into spring, it is ideal for any low-maintenance garden.

02. VIBURNUM PLICATUM
'MARIESII' JAPANESE
SNOWBALL
A showier *Viburnum* that is festooned with white lacecap flower clusters from May into June, Japanese Snowball grows in a tiered fashion, creating a wedding-cake effect.

03. VIBURNUM BURKWOODII
BURKWOOD VIBURNUM
Bundles of smaller flower clusters are formed in mid-spring. This *Viburnum* has the added benefit of scented flowers that perform brilliantly in a shadier part of the garden.

5

CLIMBERS

THAT YOU
CAN'T KILL

CHOCOLATE VINE

AKEBIA

84

CLEMATIS

CLEMATIS

88

IVY

HEDERA

92

HONEYSUCKLE

LONICERA

94

TRACHELOSPERMUM

TRACHELOSPERMUM

98

AKEBIA

CHOCOLATE VINE

——

The chocolate vine is an excellent choice for adding spring interest to a garden: a vigorous and scrambling climber that will soon spread itself over any wall or pergola you offer it. Stunning deep-purple flowers are produced from March through to May, with the addition of an unusual spicy scent that really sets it apart from other plants. It is easily one of the most eye-catching and rewarding climbers.

AKEBIA QUINATA
CHOCOLATE VINE
▼

NEED TO KNOW

—

SIZE
UP TO 12M (40FT)
(BUT DON'T LET THIS
PUT YOU OFF – IT CAN
BE EASILY MANAGED)

—

LIGHT
FULL SUN OR
PARTIAL SHADE

—

SOIL TYPE
SAND, CLAY, CHALK
OR LOAM

—

MOISTURE
MOIST BUT
WELL DRAINED

—

VARIETIES
A. quinata, chocolate
vine; *A.* 'Cream Form';
A. trifoliata, three-leaf
akebia; *A.* 'Shirobana'

WHY GROW IT

Despite its exotic and difficult appearance, the chocolate vine is actually remarkably easy to grow once you get it going. It is generally unfussy about location or soil type, and mostly concerned with just putting on a spectacular show. It is also available in a cream colour if you're looking for a climber that oozes with class. It's great in the garden and also used as a cut flower, so you can bring that unique scent into the house.

WHERE TO PUT IT

Grow it against a pergola, structure or wall in a sunny position. Just about any structure you provide will quickly become smothered in the iconic purple flowers. Plant it in a deep, fertile soil in which the roots can happily explore and spread.

HOW TO LOOK AFTER IT

As *Akebia* can eventually grow quite large if left alone, it is best to prune the plant back to size just after it has finished flowering – this can help prevent it from taking over the world! Keep it well watered, especially during the growing season, and feed it with a general-purpose slow-release fertiliser during the spring.

DO

Pick the flowers and use them to
bring the delicious scent indoors

Prune after flowering to
restrict the plant's growth

Grow two plants near each other
to encourage pollination and
enjoy the fruits produced

DON'T

Grow in a container – the plant
doesn't like its roots being disturbed

Plant against an east-facing wall – the
sun can damage any frost-caught
foliage early in the morning

Worry about pests or diseases – they
aren't normally interested in *Akebia*

THREE TO TRY

01

01. AKEBIA 'CREAM FORM'
A delightful cream version of the normally chocolate-coloured plant. It grows in a very similar way and has bronze-tinged foliage in spring. This *Akebia* will grow happily in a sunny or partially shaded spot.

02. AKEBIA TRIFOLIATA THREE-LEAF AKEBIA
Native to Japan, this is an unusual and harder to-come-by *Akebia*. Chocolate to pink flowers arrive in spring followed by rich blue fruits during the autumn, but these only appear if you grow *A. quinata* alongside.

03. AKEBIA 'SHIROBANA'
Another white-flowering *Akebia* producing masses of delicate white flowers during the spring months, which have an unusual spicy scent. These plants can be slightly harder to get hold of, but are well worth the wait if you manage to locate them!

02

03

CLEMATIS

An icon of the cottage garden, you can rely on *Clematis* to put on a display. It's possible to have a *Clematis* that will flower every month of the year. Adorned with delicate-looking flowers, it is breathtakingly beautiful and it is an incredibly resilient and easy-to-grow plant, ideal for covering an ugly wall or simply for adding height to a flower border.

CLEMATIS ARMANDII
'APPLE BLOSSOM'
ARMAND CLEMATIS
▼

—

SIZE
UP TO 8 M (26 FT) TALL

—

LIGHT
FULL SUN

—

SOIL TYPE
SAND, CLAY, CHALK
OR LOAM

—

MOISTURE
MOIST BUT
WELL DRAINED

—

VARIETIES
C. armandii 'Apple Blossom',
Armand clematis; *C. alpina*,
Austrian clematis;
C. 'Bill MacKenzie';
C. 'Polish Spirit'

WHY GROW IT

There is a *Clematis* for every month of the year, so there is no excuse not to include one in your garden. Evergreen options are a great solution for screening unsightly walls and the abundance of classy flowers, ranging from whites to dark purple, makes them a welcome addition to any garden.

WHERE TO PUT IT

Plant it by your front door to be welcomed home by the abundance of blossom-like flowers and incredible scent. Ideally, find a sunny spot on a south-facing wall for it to establish and thrive but, equally, it can tolerate some shade. Clematis grow best in the ground wherever possible.

HOW TO LOOK AFTER IT

Varieties such as 'Apple Blossom' don't require any regular pruning, so that's one less thing to worry about. However, if it does start to become too big for the space you have, you can prune it back just after flowering. Keep it well watered, and mulch and feed during the spring months with a general, balanced, slow-release fertiliser that will help it stay happy and healthy.

DO

Apply a generous mulch around the
base of the plant in early spring

Grow in a sunny position for
the best results

Use a general slow-release fertiliser
in early spring

DON'T

Worry about pruning unless
it is becoming too large

Eat it – all parts of the plant are toxic

Plant it in an exposed position – a
sheltered, sunny spot is much better

THREE TO TRY

01

02

03

01. *CLEMATIS ALPINA*
AUSTRIAN CLEMATIS
The Austrian clematis grows to
3m (10ft) but can be managed.
It produces hundreds of small,
bobbing, soft-purple flowers
throughout April and May. Ideal
for a north- or east-facing garden.

02. *CLEMATIS* 'BILL MACKENZIE'
This *Clematis* is smothered in
bright, cheerful yellow flowers
throughout the whole of summer,
followed by delicate seedheads that
last well into the winter.

03. *CLEMATIS* 'POLISH SPIRIT'
A reliable favourite in the garden
thanks to its large velvet-purple
flowers that are produced
continuously throughout summer.

HEDERA

IVY

Over the years, ivy has developed a bad reputation as the thug of the garden. But don't write off this English garden staple too quickly. Being tolerant of just about any position, not only does it add greenery that can help to soften the harshest of locations, but it is the most amazing plant to encourage wildlife, birds, bees and pollinators into the garden.

HEDERA HELIX
'GLACIER' IVY
▶

NEED TO KNOW

—

SIZE
UP TO 2.5 M (2.8 FT)

—

LIGHT
FULL SUN OR
PARTIAL SHADE

—

SOIL TYPE
CLAY, SAND, CHALK
OR LOAM

—

MOISTURE
MOIST BUT
WELL DRAINED

—

WHY GROW IT

Choose ivy for its quick growing, lush green foliage and its superb ability to attract most pollinators and wildlife into the garden. From bees to birds, it creates a unique haven for animals and insects to shelter and thrive in.

WHERE TO PUT IT

Although it grows best in a fertile, slightly alkaline soil, it will also thrive and grow just about anywhere as long it has the space to grow freely. If you have a smaller garden, there are smaller trailing options that can create the same effect.

HOW TO LOOK AFTER IT

To prevent the plants from becoming unmanageable, you can keep pruning back. This will also encourage plenty of fresh, younger growth, which can be the most impressive. Avoid pruning during nesting season (February to August) to prevent any damage to birds. During the summer months, ensure it gets plenty of water and a plant food with a high concentration of nitrogen, which will keep the foliage looking lush.

DO

Keep pruning ivy back to restrict its growth and prevent it from becoming too thuggish

Ensure it has plenty of water, especially during the summer months

Use the plant to attract wildlife and pollinators into the garden

DON'T

Prune during the bird nesting season (February to August) – it can become full of nests that you should not disturb

Plant where space is limited – many ivies are better suited to larger gardens where they have space to spread

Eat it – all parts of the plant are toxic and may cause a skin allergy

OTHERS TO TRY

—

HEDERA COLCHICA
PERSIAN IVY 'SULPHUR HEART'
Reaching up to 5m (16ft) tall, it
needs plenty of space.

■

HEDERA HELIX
'MIDAS TOUCH'
Growing to 1m (3ft), with bright
yellow foliage on red stems, this ivy
will brighten any garden.

HONEYSUCKLE

Honeysuckles are one of the most iconic, sweet-smelling climbers you can possibly grow and are a brilliant addition to any garden. They are also the perfect solution to most vertical dilemmas. Honeysuckle's fast-growing nature makes it ideal for those impatient gardeners looking for instant impact and impressive displays with minimum effort.

LONICERA
PERICLYMENUM
'GRAHAM THOMAS'
HONEYSUCKLE

▼

—

SIZE

UP TO 8M (26.2FT)

—

LIGHT

FULL SUN OR

PARTIAL SHADE

—

SOIL TYPE

SAND, CLAY, CHALK

OR LOAM

—

MOISTURE

MOIST BUT

WELL DRAINED

—

VARIETIES

L. periclymenum,

honeysuckle 'Graham

Thomas'; *L. japonica* 'Hall's

Prolific'; *L.* 'Mandarin';

L. 'Gold Flame'

WHY GROW IT

As well as looking and smelling great, honeysuckles are a superb plant for attracting pollinators into the garden. The tubular, colourful flowers produced en masse from late spring until midsummer are a brilliant attraction, not to mention the incredible aroma that will fill the garden.

WHERE TO PUT IT

Grow just about anywhere and it will still produce a prolific amount of gorgeous blooms. It is reasonably unfussy about soil type, location or aspect, although it won't grow well in deep shade. Will complement a cottage garden planting style, with its loose informal nature softening surrounding planting.

HOW TO LOOK AFTER IT

Although this plant can grow up to 8m (26ft) tall – which may seem daunting – it can also be easily managed and kept smaller through pruning. It's also worth cutting it back hard, as it has a tendency to become bare at the bottom, with all of the foliage and flowers concentrated at the top. It responds well to pruning, and with an extra mulch and some general slow-release fertiliser in the spring, it will keep rewarding you.

DO

Prune the plant back straight after flowering for better flowering the following year

Take cuttings during the autumn, a quick and easy way of getting more plants for free

Provide some support as the plant establishes – once it gets going it will cling on to anything it can find

DON'T

Use chemical sprays on the plant – this can be harmful to some wildlife

Let the plant dry out, especially during the summer months when in flower

Grow in deep shade – it needs some sun to flower and thrive

THREE TO TRY

01

01. LONICERA JAPONICA 'HALL'S PROLIFIC'
A quick growing honeysuckle that can soon reach up to 4m (13ft) tall. Masses of white tubular flowers smother the plant from spring through to summer.

02. LONICERA 'MANDARIN'
A zingy orange honeysuckle sure to brighten up any border, the foliage also has a red tinge when it first emerges during the spring – although unfortunately this is an unscented cultivar.

03. LONICERA 'GOLD FLAME'
A brilliantly scented honeysuckle with pink and orange flowers that are rather eye-catching. Flowering all summer long, it works hard for its right to be in the garden.

02

03

TRACHELOSPERMUM

Trachelospermum is one of my all-time favourite climbers. Its glossy foliage, scented flowers and autumnal colours make it a treat all year round, and the perfect climber for a sunny courtyard or patio. The divine white, star-shaped flowers will stop you in your tracks during summer.

TRACHELOSPERMUM
JASMINOIDES
CONFEDERATE
JASMINE
▼

—

SIZE

4–8M (13–26FT) TALL

—

LIGHT

FULL SUN

—

SOIL TYPE

LOAM, CHALK

OR SAND

—

MOISTURE

WELL DRAINED

—

VARIETIES

T. jasminoides,
Confederate jasmine;
T. asiaticum, Asiatic
jasmine; *T. jasminoides*
'Wilsonii', star jasmine;
T. jasminoides 'Variegatum',
confederate jasmine

WHY GROW IT

Easy to grow and yet spectacular when in flower, this climber will make your garden the envy of all your neighbours. It's also the ideal solution for covering that ugly fence or wall. It grows with vigour and determination, while its evergreen qualities make it a year-round superstar.

WHERE TO PUT IT

Find a sunny, sheltered spot in the garden with plenty of space for it to grow and mature. It thrives in a free-draining soil, so make sure it doesn't sit in water over the winter. It will happily grow in a largish container so long as you keep feeding it all year.

HOW TO LOOK AFTER IT

Feed the plant throughout the year with a general-purpose feed. This will encourage flowering and help to keep the growth lush and healthy. After the plant has finished flowering, prune back to make sure it doesn't become unmanageable and obtrusive. If left alone it can grow up to 8m (26ft) tall, but if pruned each year you can successfully keep it at the ideal size for your garden. If you're growing it in a container, pay special attention to watering and ensure it doesn't dry out during the summer.

DO

Grow up against a fence or structure to brighten up a dull area of the garden

Grow against a sunny wall for maximum flower power and to provide some protection throughout the winter months

Pinch out the tips when planting to encourage the plant to grow outwards as well as upwards

DON'T

Be afraid to keep cutting the plant back to encourage fresh growth and plenty of flowers

Grow in wet or moisture-retentive soil – free-draining soil is the key

Grow in an exposed site – it needs some protection from cold and damaging winds

THREE TO TRY

01

01. **TRACHELOSPERMUM ASIATICUM**
ASIATIC JASMINE
Similar to the commonly grown
Confederate jasmine, fragrant white
star-like flowers are produced en
masse throughout late spring and
early summer, on a backdrop of lush,
dark, glossy foliage.

02. **TRACHELOSPERMUM**
JASMINOIDES WILSONII
STAR JASMINE
Creamy white flowers are produced
on a dark green foliage with a subtle
bronze tinge. These fade to a
beautiful crisp red during the autumn.
This plant is harder to find but is still
great to grow.

03. **TRACHELOSPERMUM**
JASMINOIDES 'VARIEGATUM'
CONFEDERATE JASMINE
Variegated plants are the Marmite
of the plant world. Personally, I think
the frosty looking leaf edges add
character to the foliage and create
the perfect backdrop for the stunning
white flowers.

02

03

10

ANNUALS AND BULBS

THAT YOU
CAN'T KILL

ORNAMENTAL ONION

───

If you are looking to grow a show-stopping plant that requires no maintenance, love or affection, but will flower for up to three weeks and leave ornamental seedheads, then an ornamental onion is the one for you. Large globe-like flower clusters are produced on tall, rigid stems that elevate the blooms above other plants, allowing them to be seen in all their glory. Often found smothered in bees, this nectar-rich perennial will keep your borders full of pollinators.

ALLIUM 'GLADIATOR'
ORNAMENTAL ONION
▼

—

SIZE
UP TO 1.2M (4FT) TALL

—

LIGHT
FULL SUN

—

SOIL TYPE
SAND OR LOAM

—

MOISTURE
MOIST BUT
WELL DRAINED

—

VARIETIES
A. 'Gladiator',
ornamental onion;
A. 'Purple Sensation';
A. 'Mont Blanc';
A. amethystinum
'Red Mohican',
amethyst allium

WHY GROW IT

The compact green buds explode to reveal the star-like flowers. The large bulbs are widely available from September onwards, and each bulb will produce a single flower stem, so bear this in mind when buying – sometimes more is more!

WHERE TO PUT IT

Allium is a plant synonymous with the cottage garden but will happily lend itself to being grown in a variety of locations. It is best grown through other plants, so the dying foliage can be hidden as the plants begin to fade. Find a spot that benefits from full sun and good drainage. The slender nature of the flower stems means that this *Allium* takes up minimal space, and so lends itself well to smaller gardens.

HOW TO LOOK AFTER IT

Plant the bulbs in the autumn and, as a rule of thumb, plant them at a depth of around four times the diameter of the bulb, typically around 25cm (10in) deep. The bulbs will awaken with a bang in early spring, before erupting into flower. When this happens, the plant's energy is redirected to the flowers and the foliage can become tatty. There is no harm in removing the old leaves to prevent them detracting from the flowers. Cut back the spent stems in summer.

DO

Make sure you plant the bulbs deep enough – the deep planting encourages the bulbs to flower

Plant among other perennials that will supply lower ground cover and interest to complement the alliums

Plant in drifts; they look great en masse – just ensure that they are well spaced out

DON'T

Cut back the flower stems – the skeletons can last for months after the flowers have faded and provide great architecture

Plant in waterlogged soil – they need good drainage to become well established

Grow in the same soil in which onions have previously been grown

THREE TO TRY

01.

01. *ALLIUM* 'PURPLE SENSATION'
A great all-round *Allium* that will produce reliable, deeply coloured flower heads from mid-May onwards. Grows to around 40cm (16in) tall – a great option for pots and containers.

02. *ALLIUM* 'MONT BLANC'
A delightful, pure white *Allium* that adds style to the late spring border. Great used as dried flowers and combined with purple alliums for a more textured display.

03. *ALLIUM AMETHYSTINUM* 'RED MOHICAN' AMETHYST ALLIUM
Something slightly different that is sure to grab attention, 'Red Mohican' is a twist on a classic. With vivid scarlet blooms, which sport a rather odd mohican-style tuft from the centre, it is the punk of the *Allium* world.

02

03

CENTAUREA

CORNFLOWER

The cornflower is a very special plant for me personally, as it's the first plant I ever grew as a child. With just some compost, yoghurt pots and a packet of seeds, I became enticed by the 'real-life magic' of watching a tiny seed germinate, grow and flower. Cornflowers really are one of life's simple pleasures: understated, humble and yet a powerful component in any cutting garden thanks to their longevity and vase life.

CENTAUREA CYANUS
CORNFLOWER
▼

NEED TO KNOW

—

SIZE
UP TO 75CM (30IN)

—

LIGHT
FULL SUN

—

SOIL TYPE
SAND OR LOAM

—

MOISTURE
WELL DRAINED

—

VARIETIES
C. cyanus, cornflower;
C. cyanus 'Black Ball';
C. cyanus 'Red Boy;
C. cyanus 'Blue Boy'

WHY GROW IT

One of the easiest and most fun plants to grow from seed, the cornflower flowers continuously all through the summer months. The flowers are small and jewel-like, and do not demand attention or affection. Instead, they quite happily carry on in their own happy way. As well as being used as cut flowers, cornflowers can be dried to add something extra to Christmas bouquets.

WHERE TO PUT IT

Good drainage and full sun are the key to success with cornflowers. The sapphire-blue flowers look great grown en masse, so if you've got the space, consider converting part of your lawn or garden into a wild meadow area where they can naturalise (establish) and become a haven for wildlife. Cornflowers are also superb in pots, and essential to any cottage garden.

HOW TO LOOK AFTER IT

There really is very minimal maintenance required once the cornflower has germinated and started growing. Although you can start them off inside, they perform just as well if sown directly into the ground outdoors from May onwards. Make sure the soil is well prepared by breaking up any large clumps and creating a fine tilth (prepared surface soil) with a rake. Scatter the seeds on the soil surface and watch them emerge within a few weeks. Keep an eye out for any slug or snail damage in the first month and any competing weed seedlings if germinated directly into the soil.

DO

Grow from seed – it's dead easy and great fun

Grow cornflowers with children – they will love the bright blue flowers

Keep deadheading the flowers for successional blooms throughout the summer

DON'T

Grow in shade – cornflowers love the sun, so plant them in a nice warm position

Be too loving – cornflowers thrive on neglect and will establish well without too much TLC

Plant in clay – a very free-draining, sandy soil is ideal

THREE TO TRY

01

02

03

COSMOS

Cosmos is the princess of the cut-flower garden and queen of the container. A fantastic annual that will bloom relentlessly from June through to the first frosts. Rapidly growing into large clumps, they can quickly fill gaps in borders while maintaining their elegance and chic composure, taking the form of a cloud of flowers.

COSMOS BIPINNATUS
'CANDY STRIPE'
COSMOS
▼

SIZE
UP TO 1M (3FT) TALL

—

LIGHT
FULL SUN

—

SOIL TYPE
SAND, CHALK, CLAY
OR LOAM

—

MOISTURE
MOIST BUT
WELL DRAINED

—

VARIETIES
C. bipinnatus
'Candy Stripe';
C. 'Purity';
C. 'Double Click
Cranberries';
C. 'Rubenza'

WHY GROW IT

No summer garden is complete without a clump of *Cosmos* generously billowing over the garden path. It is the perfect plant to soften any space, no matter how big or small. The abundance of flowers is great for attracting pollinators and is ideal for cutting for use inside the home.

WHERE TO PUT IT

Unfussy about what soil they grow in, *Cosmos* prefer a position in full sun where possible. They lend themselves to being grown in containers and look truly sumptuous in an old terracotta pot on a patio. Place the larger varieties such as 'Purity' (see 'Three to try') towards the back of borders, where they can have room to grow and happily spread.

HOW TO LOOK AFTER IT

Sow seeds indoors from March to April. Sow into biodegradable pots so you can plant the plants straight out into the garden when ready without having to disturb the root system. Plant outdoors once the last frost has passed and the weather is warmer, typically from the end of May onwards. Keep deadheading and feeding the plants throughout the summer for continuous blooms. As *Cosmos* can grow quite large, it can often be good to stake the plants with old birch stems to prevent the plants from collapsing in heavy rain.

DO

Sow the seeds under cover in March or April to give the plants a head start

Pinch out the growing tips to create bushier and more compact plants

Keep harvesting the flowers throughout the summer months and remove spent flowerheads to prolong flowering and keep the display fresh

DON'T

Grow in shade – this annual thrives on full sun

Let it dry out during the summer months – this can stress the plant and cause it to become susceptible to pests and diseases

Plant out too early – wait for the weather to warm up first and gradually acclimatise the plants to the outdoors by moving them outside during the day (bringing them back inside at night) for a week before planting

THREE TO TRY

01

01. COSMOS 'PURITY'
'Purity' flowers prolifically, producing pure white flowers with a strong yellow centre. Growing to 1.2m (4ft), it makes a perfect addition to calm and neutralize strong colours.

02. COSMOS 'DOUBLE CLICK CRANBERRIES'
The petals of this double-flowering *Cosmos* create a rich ruffled effect in a deep claret colour. This *Cosmos* grows to 1m (3ft) tall and is smothered in flowers all summer.

03. COSMOS 'RUBENZA'
'Rubenza' produces flowers that are the darkest red of all the *Cosmos*. Growing to 75cm (30in), it is also one of the shortest, meaning it doesn't need staking and is perfect for container growing.

02

03

CALIFORNIA POPPY

The California poppy is a long-distance family friend of the common poppy (see page 136) we all know and love. Its bright, cheery and inspiring flowers will shine within a flowerbed or container from May through to July. *Eschscholzia* is a plant that wants to be seen and appreciated, working hard to put on a show that brings a smile to anyone's face. It's the ultimate 'anyone can grow' plant, which will keep children, adults and bees entertained from spring through to summer.

ESCHSCHOLZIA
CALIFORNICA
CALIFORNIA POPPY
▼

SIZE
UP TO 30CM (12IN)
—

LIGHT
FULL SUN
—

SOIL TYPE
SAND OR LOAM
—

MOISTURE
WELL DRAINED
—

VARIETIES
E. californica,
California poppy;
E. 'Ivory Castle';
E. 'Orange King';
E. 'Red Chief'

WHY GROW IT

We all need brighter colours in our lives. The uplifting and dazzling display produced by this easy-to-grow annual makes it a must for any low-maintenance garden looking to add a splash of summer excitement. Simple yet striking cup-shaped flowers are produced atop fine blue-grey foliage. Thriving in the toughest of conditions, the plant has a tendency to self-seed into paving and spread across the garden – not a bad trait for something so beautiful.

WHERE TO PUT IT

The California poppy is great for exposed sites that are open to the elements: a gravel or dry garden would be ideal. The plants love open drainage and somewhere they can root down easily without risk of becoming waterlogged. They make a great addition to a meadow, complementing cornflowers with a summery zing that will last well into August.

HOW TO LOOK AFTER IT

Sow seeds directly outdoors in April. They don't need to be started indoors and can simply be scattered into well-raked ground. Water well as they begin to establish, but then just leave them to it. As the first wave of blooms fade, you can remove the spent flowers to encourage a second burst.

DO

Grow from seed – they are easy to get going

Use for locations that can be affected by drought

Plant alongside blue flowers for an uplifting and summery planting combo

DON'T

Plant in the shade – they thrive in full sun and hot weather

Enrich the ground too much – they need a poor soil to establish and grow

Cut back all the seedheads in the autumn – let them self-sow and spread to become established for the following year

THREE TO TRY

01

01. *ESCHSCHOLZIA* *'IVORY CASTLE'*
A softer, more dulcet tone compared to its flamboyant sisters, 'Ivory Castle' is a lovely soft cream colour and works fantastically mingled with grasses.

02. *ESCHSCHOLZIA* *'ORANGE KING'*
As you may expect, 'Orange King' is as bold and as bright as they come. Vivid orange flowers become magnets for pollinators and bring joy to the garden.

03. *ESCHSCHOLZIA* *'RED CHIEF'*
A majestic scarlet-coloured cultivar that knows how to catch your attention. The vivid red is a powerful addition to any pots or containers, and the plant works great as a cut flower.

02

03

SUNFLOWER

Synonymous with warm summery weather and considered by many to be a quintessential plant of the cut-flower border, sunflowers originate from the Americas, but these hardy annuals do equally well in cooler climates.

—

SIZE
BETWEEN 40cm
(16in)AND 3m
(10ft) HIGH

—

LIGHT
FULL SUN

—

SOIL TYPE
ANY

—

MOISTURE
WELL DRAINED

—

VARIETIES
H. annuus, sunflower;
H. annuus 'Giant Yellow';
H. annuus 'Waooh';
H. annuus 'Ms Mars'

WHY GROW IT

They are one of the easiest annual plants to grow and will give you a bright, colourful display that will last throughout summer for no more than the price of a packet of seeds. We all know the huge varieties that grow up to 3m (10ft) high, with flowerheads larger than dinner plates. However, there are lots of smaller ones to try, some only reaching about knee height, some producing a multitude of smaller flower heads in a range of different colours. Some have coloured foliage, too.

WHERE TO PUT IT

As their name implies, sunflowers are sun dwellers and like to be in a warm, sunny spot to enable them to make their rapid growth. They can be grown in large containers and pots filled with general purpose compost but are usually grown directly in the ground. They look good in the back of a subtropical border with brightly coloured plants such as cannas, dahlias and lilies. Sunflowers also grow well in amongst vegetable plants. Plant them in amidst sweetcorn, pumpkins or courgettes, or allow climbing plants such as peas and beans to climb up their tall stems.

HOW TO LOOK AFTER IT

There are two ways to get a sunflower started, both by seed. The first method is to sow individual seeds into a 9cm (3.5in) pot in April or May, keeping them well watered on a sunny windowsill until they are about 10cm (4in) high, when they can be transplanted outside. The second method is to sow seeds directly into the ground at a spacing of 30cm (12in) in spring. As the plants grow, they will need to be kept well watered and taller varieties should be supported.

DO

Grow in full sun and use a stout stake
to support tall varieties

Sow in spring, either into pots
or directly into the ground

DON'T

Cut the flowerheads down after
flowering at the end of the season –
leave for the birds

Forget to water them every so often
during dry periods

THREE TO TRY

**01. *HELIANTHUS ANNUUS*
'GIANT YELLOW'**
Picture a sunflower; this is exactly what 'Giant Yellow' looks like. The most iconic, bold, dinner plate sized flowerheads demand attention and tower above the flower border.

**02. *HELIANTHUS ANNUUS*
'WAOOH'**
This is a smaller sunflower which is ideal for balconies or patios, producing multiple heads of bright, golden flowers that will continue to bloom right throughout the summer and into September.

**03. *HELIANTHUS ANNUUS*
'MS MARS'**
A slightly more unusual sunflower, boasting deep ruby red flowers that are sure to attract attention. It is smaller-growing, so is ideal for anyone who has less room or wants to grow it in a container.

01

02

03

DAFFODIL

The daffodil is an icon of the spring garden and a plant we all know and love, no matter how green our fingers. It provides a true sign that the winter is drawing to a close, as the cheery trumpets emerge from the cold ground. Putting on a show that can last for weeks, and ranging in colours, shapes, sizes and textures to provide interest from February right the way through to the beginning of May, there is so much to love about this reliable and consistent bulb.

NARCISSUS,
DAFFODIL
▼

SIZE
VARIES – MOST WILL
GROW UP TO 50CM
(20IN) TALL

—

LIGHT
FULL SUN OR
DAPPLED SHADE

—

SOIL TYPE
SAND, CHALK,
CLAY OR LOAM

—

MOISTURE
MOIST BUT
WELL DRAINED

—

VARIETIES
Narcissus, daffodil;
N. 'Rip van Winkle';
N. 'Tête-à-tête';
N. 'Thalia'

WHY GROW IT

The cheap bulbs are readily available from any garden centre or nursery from the end of August. No matter how big or small your garden, you can make an effort to grow these spring gems, which bring happiness and a smile to all.

WHERE TO PUT IT

Daffodils are tolerant of most conditions, but they don't want to sit in soil that is too wet. A good free-draining soil that can hold some moisture would be ideal. Banks, slopes, meadows, flower borders and containers all make great options. Basically, plant them anywhere, just make sure you plant them somewhere.

HOW TO LOOK AFTER IT

Plant the bulbs in September or October, at approximately two-and-a-half times their own depth. The key to ensuring daffodils produce continuous blooms for years on end is to make sure the bulbs are fed and not allowed to become exhausted. To do this, leave the foliage after flowering until it completely dies back. This can look unsightly for a few weeks but is well worth it for the following year's display. A good feed as the foliage begins to emerge, before the flowers appear, will also be appreciated. A diluted seaweed fertiliser would be ideal.

DO

Use them as cut flowers – bring them into the home or share them with friends

Grow in pots – they grow extremely well in containers, making them ideal for small spaces

Use to brighten up lawns – not only does this save on mowing, which should only be done once they have faded, but it creates a beautiful display throughout the spring months, far superior (in my opinion) to a finely mown lawn

DON'T

Cut back the foliage after flowering – allow it to die down and return key nutrients back to the bulbs for the following year

Dig up the bulbs – they are fine left in the ground from year to year

Eat them – daffodils are poisonous, and should not be eaten

THREE TO TRY

01

02

01. *NARCISSUS* **'RIP VAN WINKLE'**
An unusual and slightly quirky daffodil that is still easy to grow but with a dahlia-type flower that sets it apart. These flower slightly earlier, from February through to March.

02. *NARCISSUS* **'TÊTE-À-TÊTE'**
Growing to only 15cm (6in), this is a small, fun daffodil that is brilliant for growing in smaller spaces. Superb grown in containers, it gives you a splash of yellow from March to April.

03. *NARCISSUS* **'THALIA'**
An abundance of pure white trumpets are produced from March to April, adding a splash of class to mixed daffodil planting. Growing to 40cm (16in), it is a slightly larger cultivar that knows how to put on a show.

03

NIGELLA (LOVE-IN-A-MIST)

This is a truly sublime and delicate annual that creates clouds of sky-blue flowers all summer long. Living up to its common name of 'love-in-a-mist', this easy-to-grow plant produces hundreds of star-like flowers upon a light and airy foliage, which creates the illusion that they are floating. It is possibly one of the easiest annuals to grow and a must-have for any cutting garden.

NIGELLA DAMASCENA
NIGELLA
(LOVE-IN-A-MIST)
▼

—

SIZE
UP TO 50CM (20IN)
TALL, BUT BUSHY

—

LIGHT
FULL SUN

—

SOIL TYPE
SAND, CHALK
OR LOAM

—

MOISTURE
WELL DRAINED

—

VARIETIES
N. damascena,
love-in-a-mist;
N. 'Miss Jekyll';
N. 'Double White';
N. 'Deep Blue'

WHY GROW IT

The flowers are simple, romantic and dreamy – a great addition to the garden or vase. Love-in-a-mist is reliable and seldom has any growing problems, making it ideal for low-maintenance gardens that require something to bulk up flowerbeds.

WHERE TO PUT IT

This quick-growing annual loves a nice, open, sunny position where it can spread out and fill in gaps in a border. Good drainage and an open spot are key for it to establish well and produce the dazzling display that it longs to show off. Although it can grow quite large, love-in-a-mist will grow well in a large pot or container in a sunny position.

HOW TO LOOK AFTER IT

This is a simple and straightforward plant to grow, once you get it going. For best results, sow direct into a well-raked seedbed. Water well as the seedlings emerge and consider supporting the plants with some birch twigs as they grow to stop them from flopping in heavy rain. As the flowers finish, leave them to go to seed, as the ball-like seedheads are almost as impressive as the flowers themselves.

DO

Dry some cut flowers by hanging them upside down somewhere – they make great additions to winter decorations

Whilst they are flowering, keep harvesting the flowers to encourage continuous blooms

Grow in a fertile position in full sun for best results

DON'T

Grow in the shade – it loves full sun

Deadhead the flowers – the seed heads provide almost as much interest as the flowers themselves

Sow the seeds indoors – they will germinate best when sown directly where you want them to grow

THREE TO TRY

01

01. *NIGELLA* 'MISS JEKYLL'
The most commonly grown of
the *Nigella*, 'Miss Jekyll' produces
crystal-blue flowers en masse
among fine soft-green foliage.
Great for pollinators, cut flowers
and grown alongside the shorter
varieties of *Cosmos* (see page 112).

02. *NIGELLA* 'DOUBLE WHITE'
A crisp, pure-white cultivar with
a ruffled texture to the flowers,
'Double White' is a superb addition
to the cut-flower garden and great
contrasted against darker colours.

03. *NIGELLA* 'DEEP BLUE'
A deep-blue, verging on purple,
flower that grows to 60cm (24in) tall
and makes a great cut flower – bees
also adore it. Very similar to 'Miss
Jekyll', only darker in colour.

02

03

UMBEL

These plants carry their flowers in umbels: clusters of flowers on stalks, named for their distinctive umbrella-like shape. Despite their fragile appearance, they are easy to grow when you know how, and the calming white flowers add sophistication to planting. Related to carrots and cow parsley, these elegant plants are adored by wildlife.

ORLAYA GRANDIFLORA
WHITE LACEFLOWER
▼

SIZE
UP TO 75CM (30IN) TALL

—

LIGHT
FULL SUN

—

SOIL TYPE
SAND, CHALK
OR LOAM

—

MOISTURE
WELL DRAINED

—

VARIETIES
O. grandiflora, white
laceflower; *Ammi visnaga*,
toothpick bishop's weed;
Daucus carota 'Dara', wild
carrot; *Anthriscus sylvestris*
'Ravenswing'

WHY GROW IT

Umbels are perfect for the cutting garden, thanks to its romantic, lacy petals, which ooze elegance. Its drought-resistance makes it ideal for hot summers. The fine-cut foliage offers a great base from which the flowers can take centre stage.

WHERE TO PUT IT

Umbels will grow anywhere in full sun. It originates from the Mediterranean and loves the heat. Try to avoid growing the plants anywhere that they may become waterlogged or sit in water, as this will cause them to wilt and die very quickly. You can have some fun by mixing umbels among other flowering annuals to create a miniature meadow in your own garden. This is a low-maintenance, high-impact way to naturalise your garden and make it the ultimate destination for bees, butterflies and hoverflies.

HOW TO LOOK AFTER IT

Once you've got it going, the rest is easy. Sow the seeds in March or April, either in seed trays indoors or directly into the ground once the weather has warmed up properly (towards the end of April). Once the threat of frosts has passed, plant outside and mulch with some good, well-rotted compost to keep the plant snug and prevent it from drying out initially. Keep deadheading throughout the summer and it will continue to reward you prolifically.

DO

Plant alongside hardy garden *Verbena* (see page 56) in containers for a classy display all summer long

Grow from seed – it's cheaper and you'll get loads more plants to share with friends and family

Keep deadheading faded blooms to encourage continuous flowering

DON'T

Cut back the plant in the autumn – leave the flowerheads to self-seed for a continued display the following year

Grow in shade – it needs full sun to perform best

Give up on seedlings – they can take up to a month to germinate

THREE TO TRY

01

01. *AMMI VISNAGA*
TOOTHPICK BISHOP'S WEED
With delicate, finely cut foliage and
larger, more prominent umbels, this
is a fun plant to grow. The flowers
start off a lush green and open to
a pure white, creating a calming
mixture of greens and whites as the
flowers open and fade.

02. *DAUCUS CAROTA* 'DARA'
WILD CARROT
A special cultivar of the wild carrot,
with plum-tinged umbels that are
completely different to those of most
of its relatives. Grows to around
90cm (3ft) tall and flowers all
summer long.

03. *ANTHRISCUS SYLVESTRIS*
'RAVENSWING'
A delightful umbel that has brilliant
dark foliage, beautifully contrasting
with the white flowers. It is a relative
of the unruly cow parsley you may
see growing on the road verge. For
the best results, grow it from seed.

02

03

PAPAVER

POPPY

———

A symbol of peace and remembrance, this red icon is internationally famed from the battlefields of the First World War, where the artillery bombardment disturbed the soil and caused dormant poppy seeds to germinate and grow. Poppies are a large group of plants, ranging from small, dainty flowers through to large, showy blooms that pack a punch. *Papaver rhoeas* is the iconic poppy we can all recognize.

PAPAVER RHOEAS
COMMON POPPY
▾

NEED TO KNOW

—

SIZE
UP TO 75CM
(30IN) TALL

—

LIGHT
FULL SUN

—

SOIL TYPE
SAND, CHALK
OR LOAM

—

MOISTURE
WELL DRAINED

—

VARIETIES
P. rhoeas, common poppy;
P. somniferum 'Lauren's
Grape', opium poppy;
P. commutatum 'Ladybird';
P. cambricum, Welsh poppy

WHY GROW IT

As pure and simple as they come, the common poppy is easy to grow, and will thrive in the poorest of soils. Vivid red flowers are produced from May to July, or August to September depending on when they are sown. The flowers are formed of six singular petals fanning out from a black centre. When caught in the evening sun, the translucent petals glow and look spectacular.

WHERE TO PUT IT

Find a sunny position that also benefits from good drainage. Poppies like to bake in open ground and can often be found growing in farmers' fields. When the plant is happy with its position, it will readily self-seed and spread naturally, doing the hard work for you. Mix with grasses for a natural yet sophisticated combination.

HOW TO LOOK AFTER IT

Once it has got going, the rest is easy. Sow the seeds thinly across the surface of the soil and lightly rake them in. It is important not to incorporate any compost into the soil, as poppies actually prefer poor-quality soil that they can root down into. The raking will help to disturb the soil and encourage the seeds to germinate. Water well as the seedlings come through, and then leave them to create their magic. Keep deadheading to encourage continuous flowering.

DO

Disturb the soil through raking or digging to encourage the seeds to germinate

Sow the seeds on the surface of the soil and water them in well

Let poppies self-seed, spread and colonise areas of the garden

DON'T

Eat the seeds of *P. rhoeas* – it isn't one of the edible poppies!

Sow indoors – you will get the best results from seeds sown directly into the ground and left alone

Overwater – although they need some watering to help them establish, they can begin to rot if they become too wet

THREE TO TRY

01

01. *PAPAVER SOMNIFERUM*
'LAUREN'S GRAPE'
OPIUM POPPY
A rich plum-coloured poppy,
'Lauren's Grape' grows to 1m (3ft)
in height, making it much larger
than the common poppy. The
blooms are much larger, too,
and make good cut flowers.

02. *PAPAVER COMMUTATUM*
'LADYBIRD'
The 'Ladybird' poppy is a fun,
funky and slightly unusual plant
that's great to entice children into
gardening. Its red petals each have
a black polka dot, so the flower
resembles a ladybird.

03. *PAPAVER CAMBRICUM*
WELSH POPPY
The Welsh poppy is a bright and
cheerful annual that has yellow
flowers. Growing to 30cm (12in) tall,
it is compact and will happily self-
seed along a sunny driveway.

02

03

TULIP

Tulips are brilliant spring-flowering bulbs that know how to put on a show. With every colour you can possibly think of available, it's hard not to fall in love with one (or ten) to grow in your own garden. Grown in compact clusters, they are unbeatable for spring colour. In fact, during the early 1600s, tulips were so desirable that they became a form of currency in the Netherlands. At their peak, one bulb could be traded for an entire estate. Now, of course, you can pick up a bag of tulip bulbs for the same price as a nice coffee.

TULIPA 'SPRING GREEN' **TULIP**
▼

—

SIZE
UP TO 40CM
(16IN) TALL

—

LIGHT
FULL SUN

—

SOIL TYPE
SAND, CHALK
OR LOAM

—

MOISTURE
WELL DRAINED

—

VARIETIES
T. 'Spring Green';
T. 'Rococo'; *T.* 'Queen
of the Night'; *T.* 'Negrita'

WHY GROW IT

Tulips are a garden staple. A sure-sign that spring has landed and an easy way to brighten any garden, big or small. They vary in colour from soft, dulcet tones through to vibrant, bright and bold colours. They are perfect for containers on a balcony but will look just as spectacular in a large, country garden.

WHERE TO PUT IT

The ultimate container plant, nothing beats being welcomed home by a pot laden with flowering tulips, full to the brim with colour and panache. However, they will grow just as well and happily in the ground, so long as they are in a sheltered, sunny spot with plenty of drainage.

HOW TO LOOK AFTER IT

Bulbs are typically best planted in late autumn as the weather starts to become cold; they can even be planted as late as January and still put on a great performance. Tulips, although technically perennial, must conjure up so much energy to flower that they often don't come back for a second year. You can lift and store the bulbs once the foliage has died down and replant them in the autumn, but in my opinion, it is simpler and easier to keep topping up displays each autumn with additional bulbs.

DO

Plant bulbs late in the autumn – the cold weather helps prevent them from developing tulip fire (a fungal disease which makes the plants appear scorched)

Remove the spent flowers to prevent the tulips from going to seed

Plant them at a depth three times the height of the bulb

DON'T

Plant them into boggy or wet ground, as this can cause the bulbs to rot off – if in doubt, use a handful of grit when planting

Plant bulbs upside down – it sounds silly, but always plant them with the pointy side facing upwards

Remove the old foliage until it's turned completely brown – as it dies back, it returns the nutrients to the bulb and gives it the best possible chance of reflowering the following year

01

01. *TULIPA* 'ROCOCO'
A short and compact tulip, with
frilly red flowers that set it apart
from most of its relatives, 'Rococo'
is different and not afraid to shout
about it.

02. *TULIPA* 'QUEEN OF THE NIGHT'
A deep, dark and mysterious tulip.
Growing to 60cm (24in) tall, it looks
great planted among other lighter-
coloured tulips for contrast.

03. *TULIPA* 'NEGRITA'
A stylish rich-purple tulip with
closed-cup flowers that look divine
throughout April, 'Negrita' grows to
around 50cm (20in) tall.

02

03

10

FRUITS AND VEGETABLES

THAT YOU
CAN'T KILL

ALLIUM CEPA

ONION

————

A kitchen essential and garden staple, the unassuming onion must be one of the easiest vegetables you could possibly hope to grow. There are so many cultivars to choose from, each with varying strength and flavour. So whether you love a strong kick to your curry, or a sweet addition to a salad, the choice is yours.

ALLIUM CEPA
ONION
▼

SIZE
THE FOLIAGE CAN
REACH 60CM (24IN);
THE BULB, WELL,
THAT'S UP TO YOU!

—

LIGHT
FULL SUN
BUT SHELTERED

—

SOIL TYPE
SANDY LOAM,
ENRICHED WITH LOTS
OF ORGANIC MATTER

—

MOISTURE
MOIST BUT
FREE DRAINING

—

VARIETIES
A. cepa, onion; *A. cepa*
'Red Baron'; *A. cepa*
'Setton'; *A. cepa* 'Golden
Gourmet', shallot

WHY GROW IT

Onions really do just get on with it. Plant sets (baby onions) in the spring and harvest in early summer. Sets are readily available during the autumn and winter and are a great way of producing hundreds of onions for very little money.

WHERE TO PUT IT

Grow onions in full sun, somewhere they can bask in the heat, with a good, enriched soil. For big, impressive onions, plant them in the ground, where they can grow without limitation. However, to produce lots of smaller onions, plant them densely in a pot. As the foliage gets to around 30cm (12in) tall, thin out the onions, remove the papery tissue and you're left with a miniature spring onion.

HOW TO LOOK AFTER IT

Plant into well-prepared ground during the spring months. Gently push the sets into the soil, leaving just the neck sticking out of the ground. Keep them well watered, especially in the early days as they start to emerge. Onions can be hungry, so feed regularly with a general liquid fertiliser. You'll need to look out for weeds, as these will compete with the developing bulbs for water and food, meaning smaller bulbs at harvest. When the foliage starts to die back the onions are ready to harvest. Leave them in the ground for a few weeks to allow the skins to harden; this will help them keep for longer.

DO

Protect newly planted sets with netting or fleece to stop birds from uprooting them

Grow alongside mint (see page 158) to confuse and deter onion fly

Remove any flower spikes – this is referred to as the plant 'bolting', and causes the plant to put its energy into producing seed rather than a good onion

DON'T

Grow in acidic soils – they grow best in a neutral, well-drained soil

Water or feed once the foliage has died back – this means they're ready to harvest and should be left to dry out

Grow anywhere white rot or any other fungal disease has previously been – most can stay dormant in the soil and spring back to life when fresh crops are planted

THREE TO TRY

01

02

---

01. *ALLIUM CEPA* 'RED BARON'
A red onion that looks great and tastes superb. Its sweet taste makes it a brilliant addition to salads and it stores very well.

02. *ALLIUM CEPA* 'SETTON'
A popular and reliable option that produces regularly shaped, golden onions which are full of flavour.

03. *ALLIUM CEPA* 'GOLDEN GOURMET' SHALLOT
Yes, I know this isn't an onion but grow it in the same way and enjoy something different. 'Golden Gourmet' is ready for harvest from June, earlier than most onions. It is also a good option for pickling.

03

QUICK-AND-EASY ROOT VEGETABLES

Root vegetables are anything that grows under the soil, and this covers everything from carrots to parsnips, turnips to beetroot. They're ideal for containers or growing in the ground, provided you have a very free-draining light soil. A perfect solution for gardens with limited space.

RAPHANUS SATIVUS
COMMON RADISH

SIZE
VARIES BETWEEN
CROPS, BUT AS
THESE ARE ROOT
CROPS, MOST OF
THE MAGIC HAPPENS
UNDERGROUND

—

LIGHT
FULL SUN

—

SOIL TYPE
SAND OR LOAM,
FINE SOIL IS KEY

—

MOISTURE
WELL DRAINED,
MOISTURE RETENTIVE

—

VARIETIES
Daucus carota 'Early
Nantes', carrot; *Raphanus
sativus* 'Ping Pong', radish;
Beta vulgaris
'Pablo', beetroot

WHY GROW IT

Why wait for months on end for mature vegetables when the younger, quicker crops actually taste better and are easier to grow? In just a few months you can have an abundance of delicious, crisp, sweet miniature root vegetables, and all for the price of just a few packets of seeds.

WHERE TO PUT IT

The small size of these quick growing root crops makes them ideal for growing in containers or pots. Try upcycling old containers from around the home or garden. If the container has draining holes, you can grow plants in it!

HOW TO LOOK AFTER IT

If growing in the ground, rake the soil so it's nice and fine and begin sowing from late February or early March. Sow in shallow drills (small lines in the soil), cover, and water in well. As the plants grow, keep well watered and thin out any congested clumps of seedlings as they emerge. Ideally, there needs to be around 5cm (2in) between the seedlings. When harvesting, give the vegetables a quick wash and eat straight away for the best flavour.

DO

Sow new crops every few weeks
to ensure a continuous supply
throughout the growing season

Grow in pots or containers; their small
size makes them ideal for upcycling
containers around the garden

Grow onions around your carrots
to help deter carrot fly, which can
potentially ruin your crop

DON'T

Leave in the ground for too long – the
younger and smaller vegetables are
often the sweetest and tastiest

Grow in heavy soils – they require a
light, free-draining soil to thrive

Forget to water, especially
if growing in containers

THREE TO TRY

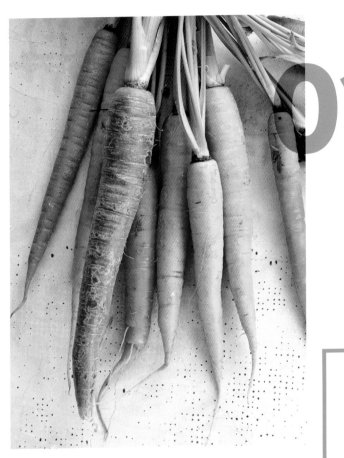

01

01. *DAUCUS CAROTA* 'EARLY NANTES' CARROT

Sow from February onwards, as this is one of the earlier carrots; they are typically ready from the beginning of June. Small, bright and crunchy carrots taste great raw as snacks.

02. *RAPHANUS SATIVUS* 'PING PONG' RADISH

Tiny balls packed with flavour and by far one of the easiest vegetables to grow. Keep sowing little and often throughout spring for a constant supply over the spring and summer.

03. *BETA VULGARIS* 'PABLO' BEETROOT

A great, early, small and quick growing beetroot. Harvest from June onwards for more succulent and tasty beets that are good used in salads or roasted.

02

03

STRAWBERRY

Synonymous with the start of summer, strawberries freshly picked from the garden have to be one of life's greatest pleasures. A world apart from anything shop bought, the unique sweet, crisp taste is indescribable, and is surely one of the greatest adverts for growing your own fruit. Just a few plants can keep you in constant supply throughout June and into July.

FRAGARIA × ANANASSA

STRAWBERRY

▾

SIZE
UP TO 30CM
(12IN) TALL

—

LIGHT
FULL SUN OR
PARTIAL SHADE

—

SOIL TYPE
SAND, CLAY, CHALK
OR LOAM

—

MOISTURE
MOIST BUT
WELL DRAINED

—

VARIETIES
F. × ananassa 'Cambridge
favourite', strawberry;
F. × ananassa 'Symphony',
strawberry; *F. × ananassa*
'Honeoye', strawberry

WHY GROW IT

With a whole catalogue of varieties to choose from, you can be sure to find one that you love. Throughout spring the plants produce simple white (or sometimes pink) daisy-like flowers with yellow centres, a delightful precursor to the fruits that follow.

WHERE TO PUT IT

Strawberries love a rich, fertile soil that is well drained. Find them a sunny position that is moderately sheltered, and they will reward you with a bounty of sweet berries. Don't restrict yourself to growing them only in the ground – be creative! Have some fun growing them in hanging baskets or containers. Even an upcycled colander can make a unique and funky planter.

HOW TO LOOK AFTER IT

These are hungry plants that require a lot of food to keep them flowering and fruiting. A tomato food is the best option, as it contains the perfect balance of nutrients. When the strawberries have finished fruiting, cut back all the old foliage to ground level to allow the plants to save energy. Not only are strawberries a perennial fruit, they also produce runners: little offshoots that create new plants. These can be cut off from the mother plant and planted to produce more fruits the following year.

DO

Keep harvesting berries daily
during the harvest season to
encourage the plants to produce
as much fruit as possible

Place straw underneath the fruits as
they form to stop them from coming
into contact with the soil and rotting

Keep feeding the plants
throughout summer to
encourage continual fruiting

DON'T

Let the birds get at your precious
crop – cover the plants with netting

Grow in windy sites where pollinators
can be kept from reaching the flowers

Plant in frost-prone areas or
anywhere that tomatoes have
previously been grown

THREE TO TRY

01

**01. *FRAGARIA × ANANASSA*
STRAWBERRY 'CAMBRIDGE
FAVOURITE'**
One of the most commonly grown
varieties – and for good reason.
Its prolific fruiting of large, flavour-
packed strawberries, good disease
resistance and reliability makes it
very popular.

**02. *FRAGARIA × ANANASSA*
STRAWBERRY 'SYMPHONY'**
A more vigorous cultivar producing
an abundance of juicy red berries,
with great flavour, throughout June
and July.

**03. *FRAGARIA × ANANASSA*
STRAWBERRY 'HONEOYE'**
'Honeoye' is often grown
commercially, thanks to its heavy
cropping and early fruiting. Its fruits
are on the small side and the plant
lends itself well to being grown in
a container.

02

03

MINT

Mint is an easy-to-grow perennial herb. So easy, in fact, it is somewhat of a maverick, a garden rebel that hates to conform to rules. It can become an escape artist given half a chance, but it can easily be controlled and utilised as a vigorous and valuable perennial. Although we are used to cooking and using just a few types of mint, there are in fact dozens of unique and wonderful cultivars and flavours to choose from.

MENTHA SPICATA
SPEARMINT
▼

—

SIZE
UP TO 80CM
(30IN) TALL

—

LIGHT
FULL SUN OR
PARTIAL SHADE

—

SOIL TYPE
SAND, CLAY, CHALK
OR LOAM

—

MOISTURE
MOIST BUT
WELL DRAINED

—

VARIETIES
M. spicata, spearmint;
Prostanthera cuneata,
Alpine mint;
M. × piperita f. *citrata*
'Chocolate'; *M. requienii*,
Corsican mint

WHY GROW IT

Everyone loves mint. Be it in a summery glass of Pimm's, a warming winter tea or a refreshing ice cream, there is a minty recipe for every occasion. In the garden, it is a small shrub of lush, aromatic foliage, with light purple flower spikes during the summer – both delicious and beautiful.

WHERE TO PUT IT

Grow mint in full sun somewhere that it can receive plenty of water. Its spreading habit means it is best grown in a pot or container, making it perfect for a balcony or patio.

HOW TO LOOK AFTER IT

If growing mint in the ground, plant it within a pot to prevent it from spreading too much. This does make the plant more susceptible to drying out but will save you a lot of time when it comes to weeding it out of unwanted places. When the plant has finished flowering, cut back hard to just above ground level to encourage a second flush of leaves. Cut it back completely over winter.

DO

Plant it within a pot to contain the roots and prevent unwanted spreading

Cut right back after flowering to encourage a flush of fresh new growth

Use the leaves straight from the plant to make a fresh mint tea – nothing can beat the taste

DON'T

Allow it to run rampant – it can spread and take over if not restricted

Let the plants dry out – they can be very thirsty, especially during summer

Grow several different mints in the same container – they can each lose their unique taste and smell

THREE TO TRY

01

01. *PROSTANTHERA CUNEATA*
ALPINE MINT
Growing to 1m (3ft) tall, the lesser-known alpine mint makes a great shrubby perennial. The foliage still has a strong minty aroma, but the leaves are much smaller and subtler.

02. *MENTHA × PIPERITA F. CITRATA* 'CHOCOLATE'
CHOCOLATE MINT
Chocolate mint produces deep-green leaves with a chocolatey scent and flavour – a great novelty that can be used in cooking and perfect for chocoholics!

03. *MENTHA REQUIENII*
CORSICAN MINT
The smallest and most delicate of all the mints, Corsican mint thrives in shady, moist conditions. The tiny foliage creates a soft, lush carpet, releasing a truckload of scent when crushed.

02

03

CUT-AND-COME-AGAIN LETTUCE

Imagine being able to hack a plant back to within an inch of its life, only for it to come back lusher, stronger and providing a constant source of delicious, free food. Well, this is indeed the case with cut and come again salads: an ingenious, fast-growing solution to keeping kitchens topped up throughout the year with the freshest, tastiest salad leaves.

LACTUCA SATIVA
LETTUCE
▼

SIZE
UP TO 20CM (8IN) TALL
—

LIGHT
FULL SUN
—

SOIL TYPE
SANDY, CLAY OR
LOAM (OR JUST
GENERAL MULTI-
PURPOSE COMPOST)
—

MOISTURE
MOIST WITH
GOOD DRAINAGE
—

VARIETIES
L. satvia, lettuce;
Eruca sativa, rocket;
Brassica juncea 'Red Giant';
Taraxacum officinalis,
dandelion

WHY GROW IT

Growing salad leaves is a great way of engaging children with the wonders of growing. From just one packet of seeds, you can expect a continuous supply of cut leaves throughout the year. Each plant can be cut back around four times before it loses energy, but by continually sowing seeds every two weeks, you'll never be short of a crunchy leaf.

WHERE TO PUT IT

Just about anywhere, be it out in the garden, in a container or even on a windowsill. These salads are unfussy about location and will be among the easiest plants you've ever grown. If you're short on space, then simply use a growing bag laid flat, expose the compost and sow the seeds straight onto the surface – easy!

HOW TO LOOK AFTER IT

You can begin to sow seeds from February onwards if you're starting them indoors on a windowsill. If sowing directly into the garden, wait until April. As they germinate, it can be worth thinning out any congested clumps of seedlings to prevent any mildew or damping off (a disease that affects seedlings) from occurring. Keep them well watered and cut regularly to ensure a constant supply. If growing them outside in the ground, it can be worth digging in extra compost or well-rotted manure to ensure the soil is lovely and rich.

DO

Harvest as and when required – that way you're guaranteed the freshest, crispest lettuce possible

Cut the leaves in the morning when they're at their freshest

Continually sow throughout the year to keep a constant supply readily available

DON'T

Let the soil dry out – this can make the lettuce bolt and go to seed (produce flowerheads)

Sow too deep – the seeds are very small and can be sown on the surface and covered with a thin sprinkling of compost

Harvest the whole plant

THREE TO TRY

01

01. *ERUCA SATIVA* ROCKET
With a peppery kick that will bring salads or pizzas to life, rocket is very easy to grow. Just make sure you keep harvesting regularly, as the fresh young leaves are the tastiest.

02. *BRASSICA JUNCEA* 'RED GIANT'
Delicious eaten raw or even cooked into stir-fries, 'Red Giant' is a strong-flavoured leaf that packs a punch: simple, easy but very powerful!

03. *TARAXACUM OFFICINALIS* DANDELION
Although it may be a weed to most people, dandelion makes a delightful addition to salads, and is rich in vitamins, minerals and phytochemicals. The flowers can also brighten up dishes, and if you keep on top of harvesting, you can prevent it from seeding into unwanted areas.

02

03

PEA

Nothing comes close to the taste of peas straight from the garden –
a revelation compared to anything you can buy in a shop. They are the
perfect addition to a meal or, even better, just enjoyed as a snack straight
from the plant.

—

SIZE
VARIES DEPENDING
ON THE VARIETY, BUT
USUALLY AROUND
1M (3FT)

—

LIGHT
FULL SUN

—

SOIL TYPE
SAND, CLAY OR LOAM

—

MOISTURE
MOIST BUT
WELL DRAINED

—

VARIETIES
P. sativum, pea; *P. sativum*
'Sugar Ann'; *P. sativum*
'Shiraz'; *P. sativum*
'Kelvedon Wonder'

WHY GROW IT

From just one small pea seed, you can expect hundreds of delicious peas. Not only will you be rewarded with an abundance of these delicious pearls, but they are a superb way to engage children with gardening.

WHERE TO PUT IT

Either grow directly in the ground or in a container, ideally somewhere in full sun that has good soil and holds plenty of moisture. The key to growing good pea plants is ensuring that they have plenty of room to stretch and grow. Allow ample space and they will reward you heavily.

HOW TO LOOK AFTER IT

A good compost or soil is essential to getting the plants going. Try digging in plenty of compost or well-rotted manure to improve the soil and help retain moisture. Once they start growing, make sure you provide some support – old twigs would be ideal – for them to clamber through. Keep the plants well watered and feed them regularly with a general liquid food.

DO

Keep continually harvesting pods for fresh and tasty peas – the more you pick, the more you will get

Pinch out the pea tips and use in salads – pinching encourages the plant to grow bushier and stronger

Leave a few pods on the plant towards the end of the season – allow these to dry and you will have your pea seeds for next year, for free!

DON'T

Let the plants dry out, especially as they start to flower

Dig out the roots in the autumn – they are amazing at capturing and adding nitrogen to the soil, a vital nutrient for leafy vegetables such as cabbages or lettuce

Let the mice steal your newly sown seeds – give the seeds a head start and pre-sow them into lengths of guttering

01

02

01. *PISUM SATIVUM* 'SUGAR ANN'
This sugarsnap pea is one of the
earlier varieties to produce pods.
It provides an abundance of sweet,
crisp pods that are divine eaten
fresh or used in stir-fries.

02. *PISUM SATIVUM* 'SHIRAZ'
A truly beautiful, vivid purple
mangetout pea. The sumptuous,
velvety pods are produced from June
onwards – keep picking the young
pods, as these have the best flavour.

03. *PISUM SATIVUM*
'KELVEDON WONDER'
Reliable and delicious, this is a first
early pea, which means it's one of
the first to start producing pods.
Great eaten raw, cooked or even
frozen and enjoyed throughout the
rest of the year.

03

ROSEMARY

A plant we've all heard of or used in our cooking, but aside from its culinary popularity, it also makes a brilliant and versatile plant for the garden. Sporting silver-green to grey foliage, which provides interest all year round, it really is hardy. From larger-growing shrub rosemary to squat trailing varieties, there is an option for any garden, no matter what size.

ROSMARINUS
OFFICINALIS
ROSEMARY

SIZE
UP TO 50cm (20in) TALL,
BUT CAN SPREAD TO
1m (3ft) WIDE

—

LIGHT
FULL SUN

—

SOIL TYPE
SAND, CHALK
OR LOAM

—

MOISTURE
WELL DRAINED

—

VARIETIES
R. officinalis, rosemary;
R. 'Prostratus Group';
R. 'Sissinghurst Blue';
R. 'Lady in White'

WHY GROW IT

What's not to love? It's easy to grow, provides year-round interest, has beautiful sky-blue flowers, is brilliant for texture, not to mention it smells superb. Rosemary is the ultimate garden plant that never stops performing. It will happily tolerate being clipped, making it a great alternative to low-growing topiary or even as structure in among summer-flowering perennials.

WHERE TO PUT IT

Grow in the sunniest position in the garden, somewhere it can really bask in the heat – after all, it does have Mediterranean origins. A dry or gravel garden would be perfect. In addition to the shrub forms, trailing varieties can be a fun addition, being grown as ground cover or allowed to tumble out of a container. This not only looks great but smells incredible when you brush past it.

HOW TO LOOK AFTER IT

As long as it's being grown somewhere dry and sunny, the rest is easy. Keep it well watered during the summer, and move plants being grown in pots into a sheltered spot during the winter months. If you spot any fluorescent beetles on the plant, remove them by hand straight away and kill them, otherwise the plant will be destroyed.

DO

Keep harvesting the leaves and using them in cooking – rosemary is best picked and added to dishes straight from the bush

Water regularly, especially during hot summers – although rosemary thrives in heat, it doesn't like to be bone dry

Grow in a pot or container – its trailing habit makes it ideal for cascading down pots

DON'T

Grow somewhere it will become waterlogged – it hates having wet feet

Cut back too hard – instead, keep cutting little and often for cooking

Grow in very fertile ground – it prefers a poorer soil

THREE TO TRY

01

01. *ROSMARINUS* 'PROSTRATUS GROUP' ROSEMARY
A trailing variety of rosemary that makes a great container plant. Grow it right by the door, so you can appreciate its incredible scent and blue flowers every day.

02. *ROSMARINUS* 'SISSINGHURST BLUE' ROSEMARY
An erect, upright rosemary that grows to around 1.5m (5ft) tall, making it a fairly good-sized shrub, 'Sissinghurst Blue' has beautiful blue flowers.

03. *ROSMARINUS* 'LADY IN WHITE' ROSEMARY
A compact rosemary that grows into a low shrub, with subtle but slightly unusual white flowers that are produced from spring through to summer.

RASPBERRY

What would our summers be without a handful of raspberries picked fresh from the garden and enjoyed on a sunny evening? For a plant that is so easy to grow, the fruit's short shelf life makes it exceedingly expensive in any supermarket. So, to save a shedload of money and double the flavour of the 'off-the-shelf' fruit, grow your own.

RUBUS IDAEUS
RASPBERRY
▼

SIZE
UP TO 1.8M (6FT) TALL
—

LIGHT
FULL SUN
—

SOIL TYPE
SAND, CLAY OR LOAM
—

MOISTURE
MOIST BUT
WELL DRAINED
—

VARIETIES
R. idaeus, raspberry;
R. idaeus 'All Gold';
R. idaeus 'Polka';
R. idaeus 'Ruby Beauty'

WHY GROW IT

Raspberries, like blackberries, are remarkably easy to grow and can produce an impressive amount of fruit for such a simple plant. There are two main groups of raspberries, to keep you picking from late July right through to the end of autumn. The simple distinction: summer-fruiting raspberries produce fruit on last year's growth, whereas autumn-fruiting raspberries produce fruit on the new growth. The only difference when growing is how and when you prune – simple!

WHERE TO PUT IT

For best results, grow in a sunny but sheltered position. Most raspberry cultivars can grow quite large, some up to 1.8m (6ft) tall, so it is often best to grow against a fence or wall that will offer suitable protection. The smaller-growing plants can be happily grown in a pot or container on a balcony or patio.

HOW TO LOOK AFTER IT

Once you've determined whether you're growing summer- or autumn-fruiting raspberries, the rest is easy. Cut back the canes (stems) that have finished fruiting on the summer-fruiting plants, leaving the unfruited stems intact. For the autumn-fruiting plants, it's even simpler: just cut all the canes back to ground level in early winter. Keep the plants well hydrated and feed every month during the growing season to help them produce as much fruit as possible. They benefit from a good mulch in early spring; compost or well-rotted horse manure is perfect.

DO

Plant during the autumn and winter as bare-root plants (with no soil around the roots) – the plants will respond better, plus it's cheaper

Dig plenty of good, well-rotted organic matter into the ground before planting

Keep continually harvesting to make sure you don't miss any of the delicious fruits

DON'T

Grow large cultivars in containers – choose a dwarf variety such as 'Ruby Beauty' (see page 177)

Let the plants dry out, especially during warmer weather

Grow in chalky or limestone soil – they can become deficient in key nutrients

THREE TO TRY

01

02

01. RUBUS IDAEUS
'ALL GOLD' RASPBERRY
Something completely different
that's sure to add interest to
summer fruit salads. Compact
plants produce golden, jewel-like
fruits that have the most incredible
flavour, which is often preferred
over most traditional favourites.

02. RUBUS IDAEUS
'POLKA' RASPBERRY
'Polka' is a traditional autumn-
fruiting plant grown for its potential
ability to produce two crops in one
year. Great-tasting fruits with a long
shelf life make it a surefire plant to
grow, but it can get quite big.

03. RUBUS IDAEUS **'RUBY
BEAUTY' RASPBERRY**
A new, small, summer-fruiting
variety that allows you to grow
raspberries even in the very
smallest of spaces.

03

POTATO

The humble spud: one of the most versatile members of the vegetable world. Potatoes are a fun and easy crop to grow. With hundreds of varieties to choose from, you are sure to find one (or several) that you love. Why not have some fun and choose unusual varieties you can't easily buy from the shops?

SOLANUM TUBEROSUM

POTATO
▼

SIZE
THE FOLIAGE CAN GROW TO AROUND 80CM (30IN) ABOVE GROUND LEVEL

—

LIGHT
FULL SUN; AVOID FROST POCKETS

—

SOIL TYPE
SANDY LOAM

—

MOISTURE
FREE DRAINING BUT MOISTURE RETENTIVE

—

VARIETIES
S. tuberosum, potato; *S. tuberosum* 'Pink Fir Apple'; *S. tuberosum* 'Charlotte'; S. *tuberosum* 'Purple Majesty'

WHY GROW IT
Freshly harvested new potatoes, boiled for ten minutes or so with a few sprigs of mint from the garden (see page 158), are a divine meal in their own right. Freshly harvested produce always tastes infinitely better than anything you can buy from the shop, and this is certainly the case with the humble potato.

WHERE TO PUT IT
Containers are a great and easy way of growing potatoes. In fact, many of the specialist show growers find that growing them in containers produces a better crop. This of course has the added benefit that you can simply tip out the container or pot when ready and save yourself having to dig. Do, however, make sure that the foliage has plenty of room to grow.

HOW TO LOOK AFTER IT
Make sure you buy your potato tubers from reputable suppliers: the best seed will help to produce the best crops. When planting your potatoes, bury them around 12cm (5in) deep, but as the foliage breaks through, keep topping them up with soil or compost until only the topmost leaves show. Keep an eye out for potato blight, which is caused in warm, wet conditions.

DO

'Chit' your potato tubers in early spring for planting mid to late spring: stick them on top of a cupboard for a few weeks and they will produce little eyes – this gives them a head start when planted

If you're feeling particularly frugal, cut the potato tubers in half to make your supplies go further

Keep covering the emerging growth with soil or compost to prevent frost damage – this is called 'earthing up'

DON'T

Leave potatoes in the ground for too long after they are ready to harvest – the slugs may beat you to them

Eat green potatoes or any of the foliage or fruit above ground – green potatoes that have been exposed to sunlight and produce tomato-like fruits are poisonous.

Let the plants dry out: the size of the potato is often directly attributed to watering – less water means smaller potatoes

THREE TO TRY

01

01. **SOLANUM TUBEROSUM 'PINK FIR APPLE' POTATO**
The original salad potato. The distinctive small, pink potatoes are ideal for boiling and have a distinctive nutty taste. They are perfect served cold in a salad on a warm summer's day.

02. **SOLANUM TUBEROSUM 'CHARLOTTE' POTATO**
'Charlotte' is a reliable and very popular second early potato. It produces small pear-shaped potatoes throughout July, and these make a great addition to salads.

03. **SOLANUM TUBEROSUM 'PURPLE MAJESTY' POTATO**
'Purple Majesty' produces heavy crops of vivid purple potatoes that not only look great and taste superb, but are actually better for you, as they're higher in beneficial anthocyanin antioxidants.

02

03

THYME

Tough, hardy and a plant that you can literally walk on to help it thrive (seriously), not only is thyme one of the most indestructible plants you could possibly grow, it also benefits from being beautiful, great for wildlife and, of course, edible. There are dozens of brilliant varieties that can be grown at home, each slightly different and varying in height, colour, texture and flavour, but they all have one thing in common: they refuse to be killed.

THYMUS VULGARIS
COMMON THYME
▼

SIZE
UP TO 15CM (6IN) TALL
—

LIGHT
FULL SUN
—

SOIL TYPE
SAND, CHALK
OR LOAM
—

MOISTURE
WELL DRAINED
—

VARIETIES
T. vulgaris, common thyme;
T. serpyllum coccineus,
creeping red thyme;
T. 'Silver Queen';
T. 'Doone Valley'

WHY GROW IT

Thymus vulgaris is the most commonly grown thyme and one of the most reliable. It flowers from May through to July, with delicate soft-pink flowers that sit just above the small, aromatic foliage. Common thyme also grows well from seed. The seeds can be sprinkled into cracks and crevices in the garden, where they will grow and soften paving.

WHERE TO PUT IT

Grow it anywhere sunny with good drainage. It is the perfect ground cover plant for a dry or gravel garden. If you want to try something fun and different, plant it densely and allow the plants to knit together to create a 'thyme lawn'. When you walk on it, it will release an incredible fragrance, and it can even be mowed to keep the plants low and compact.

HOW TO LOOK AFTER IT

The best growth for cooking is the fresh new foliage. The key to a constant production of this is to continually cut back the plants to encourage lush new growth. The more you cut thyme back, the better it will respond, and regular pruning will prevent it from becoming too woody, which can happen over time.

DO

Grow it as an alternative to grass – thyme's low-growing, compact and durable nature makes it great to walk on

Keep trimming and harvesting the plants to keep them compact and stop them from becoming woody

Use thyme to attract wildlife into the garden

DON'T

Plant it somewhere wet – it needs good drainage to thrive and survive

Grow in the shade – it loves full sun

Be afraid to cut it right back – the tougher you treat it, the stronger it will keep coming back

01

01. *THYMUS SERPYLLUM COCCINEUS*
CREEPING RED THYME
One of the lowest-growing thymes,
creeping red thyme just hugs the floor.
It is one of the most popular varieties
to grow, producing a profusion of
small pink flowers for months on end.

02. *THYMUS* 'SILVER QUEEN'
THYME
A slightly larger-growing thyme,
growing up to 20cm (8in) tall, which
can become slightly woody with time.
It has lush silver-tinged variegated
foliage that can be used to lighten
up surrounding planting.

03. *THYMUS* 'DOONE VALLEY'
THYME
'Doone Valley' is a golden thyme
that adds a splash of sunshine to
the garden. Growing very low to the
ground, it won't get taller than 10cm
(4in). Mix with other thymes to
create a tapestry effect.

10

HOUSE PLANTS

THAT YOU
CAN'T KILL

CAST IRON PLANT

ASPIDISTRA ELATIOR

188

ALOE

ALOE

192

CACTI

CACTACEAE

196

FRIENDSHIP TREE

CRASSULA

200

FIDDLE-LEAF FIG

FICUS

204

SWISS CHEESE PLANT

MONSTERA DELICIOSA

208

UMBRELLA TREE

SCHEFFLERA

210

HOUSELEEK

SEMPERVIVUM

212

PEACE LILY

SPATHIPHYLLUM WALLISII

216

AIR PLANT

TILLANDSIA

218

CAST IRON PLANT

___

As its common name suggests, this plant is as indestructible as they come and will tolerate much neglect. This makes it an ideal starter plant for anyone who is slightly nervous about giving house plants a go and unsure about growing something more tropical and demanding. Originating from the forests of China and Japan, in its natural habitat *Aspidistra* spreads along the woodland floor. In cooler climates, however, it is much more comfortable being protected from the elements.

ASPIDISTRA ELATIOR
CAST IRON PLANT
▼

SIZE
UP TO 50cm
(20in) TALL

LIGHT
FULL TO
PARTIAL SHADE

—

SOIL TYPE
WELL-DRAINED
HOUSE PLANT
COMPOST

—

MOISTURE
WELL DRAINED

—

VARIETIES
A. elatior, common
cast iron plant;
A. elatior 'Okame'

WHY GROW IT

Aspidistra is grown mainly for its deep, straplike and shiny evergreen leaves that look great all year round. It is a brilliant foliage plant that can withstand most conditions, making it invaluable in the world of house plants. Although it won't produce flowers or change during the course of the year, the simplicity of the lush green leaves makes it interesting enough in its own way.

WHERE TO PUT IT

Although the plant will happily grow in most locations, if you can, try and grow it in semi-shade: somewhere out of direct sunlight but, equally, not in the deepest, darkest corner of the room. *Aspidistra* is a very commonly grown office plant, softening desks and greening up work environments – something that is proven to make us more productive.

HOW TO LOOK AFTER IT

Although the cast iron plant is very easy to grow and tolerant of most conditions, it does still like a bit of love from time to time. Keep it constantly watered throughout the summer months and reduce watering during the winter. As leaves begin to deteriorate and become tatty, cut them right back to the soil and fresh new foliage will begin to emerge.

DO

Leave it alone and relax – this is one of the most undemanding plants you could hope to grow

Avoid growing the plant on a windowsill – the direct sunlight and strong heat can stress and scorch the plant

Give the plant good drainage – use gravel or clay pebbles as a base layer to help improve drainage through the pot and prevent it from sitting wet

DON'T

Overwater – although it does require regular watering during the summer months

Grow in direct sunlight – this can scorch the leaves

Over-pot – they can last for many years in the same pot and don't mind being a bit pot-bound (where the roots fill the pot)

TWO TO TRY

01

01. ***ASPIDISTRA ELATIOR***
    COMMON ASPIDISTRA
    The most commonly grown
    Aspidistra, and for good reason:
    its immensely tough, resilient
    foliage can grow in just about
    any space. However, it thrives
    best in a shady spot.

02. ***ASPIDISTRA ELATIOR*** 'OKAME'
    For fans of something slightly
    more unusual, this variegated
    Aspidistra will brighten up any
    shady corner with a spectacular
    display of brilliantly striped foliage.

02

ALOE

Aloe is a key ingredient in many cosmetic products. In addition to its healing and skincare properties, however, *Aloe* also makes a fantastic addition to the home as a very easy-to-grow and difficult-to-kill house plant. It's a succulent that is ideal for those who are a touch forgetful when it comes to watering.

ALOE VERA

BARBADOS ALOE

▼

WHY GROW IT

Large, thick and fleshy leaves bring structure and architecture to the home. *Aloe* is an evergreen plant that will provide interest throughout the year, and mature plants can also produce the most amazing bright yellow flowers, similar to those of a red-hot poker. The foliage is a soft-green colour, with subtle white markings along the surface.

WHERE TO PUT IT

Aloe likes a sunny location, such as a south-facing windowsill, where it can bask in the heat and light. If possible, try to avoid the plant becoming scorched during the midday sun, although it can tolerate this if necessary. Don't grow it in a shady position or around more tropical plants that require a higher humidity.

HOW TO LOOK AFTER IT

Allow the plant to completely dry out in between watering. Remember: the large, fleshy leaves store and hold a lot of water, so the plant can keep itself going for weeks on end and doesn't need to be continually flooded. Grow it in a very free-draining compost and mix in plenty of grit when potting.

DO

Grow in a sunny position on a south-facing windowsill

Take your aloes outside during the warm summer months – the good airflow will be great for the plants and you can enjoy them in a totally different setting

Use the sap straight from the leaves on any burns or dry skin – it works wonders, and is much cheaper than buying *Aloe vera* skin creams

DON'T

Overwater – allow the plants to dry out completely in between watering

Grow in shade, as *Aloe vera* requires full sun to thrive and become well established – remember, it is a succulent

THREE TO TRY

01

01. *ALOE ARISTATA* LACE ALOE
A commonly grown *Aloe*, ideal for
the windowsill. Dense, juicy foliage
in a greeny-grey shade will happily
bask in full sunshine and, if really
happy, will produce bright orange
flower stems.

02. *ALOE VERA* BARBADOS ALOE
The *Aloe* you are most likely to have
heard of, grown or used on your skin.
It has dense clusters of thick, juicy
foliage. In tropical regions, it can
produce immensely beautiful flower
spikes but in most other locations
it remains a foliage only plant.

03. *ALOE POLYPHYLLA*
MANY-LEAVED ALOE
This is such a cool plant, and its
low spiral rosette of tightly packed
foliage makes it the perfect coffee
table centrepiece.

02

03

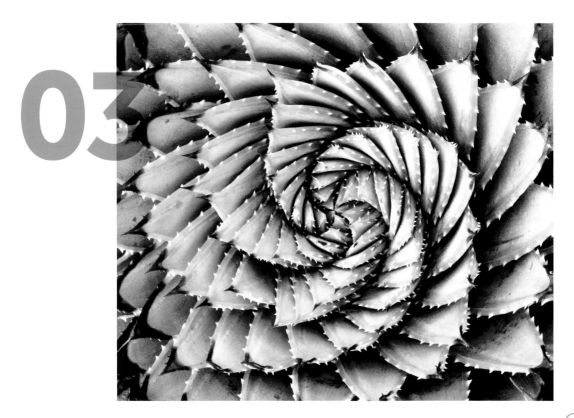

The most forgiving of all the house plants, cacti not only survive neglect but thrive on it. They may appear to be unassuming, even ugly, plants, outcasts of the plant world, but in fact they are brilliant examples of plant innovation and evolution. They have adapted over thousands of years to tolerate and establish in the very toughest of conditions, meaning that your windowsill isn't going to be too challenging for these resilient and robust house plants.

CACTACEAE

CACTI

▼

SIZE
VARIES DEPENDING
ON THE SPECIES
—

LIGHT
FULL SUN
—

SOIL TYPE
A FREE-DRAINING
AND GRITTY
COMPOST MIXTURE
—

MOISTURE
WELL DRAINED
—

VARIETIES
Echinopsis, hedgehog
cactus; *Cereus,* cereus;
Opuntia, prickly pear

WHY GROW IT

Cacti have the amazing ability to store water – the camels of the plant world, if you like. Their spines are carefully positioned to minimise water loss, and these clever plants are designed to be virtually indestructible.

WHERE TO PUT IT

Find the sunniest, driest spot in your home, with good airflow. Cacti don't want to be grown close to other more tropical house plants, as the misting and transpiration from humidity-loving neighbours can cause problems for the cacti. A south-facing windowsill would be ideal.

HOW TO LOOK AFTER IT

Leave them to it. Most cacti that die are killed through receiving too much love and care; they much prefer to just be left alone and watered only when the soil has completely dried out. Remember, they naturally grow in deserts, where rains can be weeks apart. If the plants need repotting, do so in spring, and plant only into a slightly larger pot. Wrap the plant in a tea towel or similar first to protect yourself from the vicious spines. Use a very free-draining compost.

DO

Allow the plants to dry out completely before rewatering

Grow in a very free-draining compost and use plenty of grit when repotting

Be extremely careful when handling the plants – the spines may not look like much, but they can give you a serious prick

DON'T

Allow the plants to sit in water – they will rot very quickly

Grow close to a window during winter – the cold weather can damage the plants

Grow in an area with high humidity – this can cause cacti to rot away; they much prefer hot, dry conditions with very good airflow

THREE TO TRY

01

01. *ECHINOPSIS*
HEDGEHOG CACTUS
The hedgehog cactus is most probably the plant you immediately think of when you hear the word 'cactus'. Native to South America, they form large, globe-like cushions with small white spines.

02. *CEREUS* CEREUS
Native to South America, *Cereus* cacti will thrive in a sunny location with good drainage. The key characteristics of these cacti are their uniquely ridged stems and night-flowering blooms.

03. *OPUNTIA* PRICKLY PEAR
The prickly pear can be grown outdoors if you are able to provide suitable winter protection and prevent the ground from becoming too wet. However, it is much easier to grow it indoors on a sunny windowsill. Be careful – this unassuming plant can be very painful if you touch it.

02

03

FRIENDSHIP TREE

The friendship tree is a brilliant house plant that loves to bask in a sunny position. It's one of those plants that you can generally forget about, only to be rewarded with a brilliant display of succulent foliage. Unfortunately, despite its alternative name of 'money plant', it doesn't actually produce any money, but it does keep on effortlessly providing handsome greenery throughout the year.

CRASSULA OVATA
FRIENDSHIP TREE
▼

—

SIZE
UP TO 2M (6.5FT) TALL
(BUT IT SELDOM
REACHES THIS
SIZE INDOORS)

—

LIGHT
FULL SUN

—

SOIL TYPE
GRITTY, FREE-
DRAINING HOUSE
PLANT COMPOST

—

MOISTURE
WELL DRAINED

—

VARIETIES
C. ovata, money
plant, jade plant or
friendship tree; *C. ovata*
'Gollum'; *C. schmidtii*

WHY GROW IT

Most *Crassula* have plump, glossy, evergreen leaves are slightly oval, and have a brilliant red tinge to the edges. The leaves are produced on woody stems that give the plant the appearance of a small and compact tree. It will grow as big or small as you want it to be.

WHERE TO PUT IT

Find the sunniest spot in your house, be it a windowsill or a coffee table that benefits from plenty of sunlight throughout the day. Avoid growing it directly next to a cold window, where the plant can suffer from the low temperatures, or by a door where a draught might cause it stress. A south-facing location is ideal.

HOW TO LOOK AFTER IT

The plant's size is completely controlled by the size of the pot that it is growing in: the bigger the pot, the larger the plant. Equally, if you want to keep the plant small and cute, then grow it within a small container. Water sparingly through the summer and reduce the frequency of watering completely during the winter months. As a succulent, the money plant can very easily be overwatered. The plant actually retains moisture in the summer months, storing it for the winter when, curiously, it does most of its growing.

DO

Use a plant tonic on
the foliage – this will help to
stop insect attacks

Avoid watering completely during
the winter months

Grow new plants from leaf cuttings –
simply remove a leaf, let it dry out for
a few days so that the wood hardens,
and push the end into a pot of
free-draining compost

DON'T

Overwater – although it does
require some water, especially
during the summer months, it is
important to make sure that the
water can drain away quickly

Grow in a heavy soil – a free-draining
house plant mixture is ideal

Grow too near to a cold
window, especially during
the cold winter months

CRASSULA
THREE TO TRY

01

02

01. ***CRASSULA OVATA* 'GOLLUM'**
Similar to the normal *Crassula*, only it has cupped, curled edges at the tips, almost mimicking the leaves of a carnivorous plant.

02. ***CRASSULA OVATA* FRIENDSHIP TREE, JADE PLANT OR MONEY PLANT**
The most common *Crassula*, with beautiful red-tinged, plump, fleshy foliage and a continual desire to thrive throughout neglect and drought.

03. ***CRASSULA SCHMIDTII***
Much narrower, pointed foliage forms a low cushion of dense cover. The flowers are the standout feature, with rosy pink blooms formed throughout the winter months and into spring.

03

FIDDLE-LEAF FIG

——

Figs are among the all-time favourite house plants. Their dominant, glossy, evergreen foliage can add structure to indoor planting, while the plants are incredibly easy to grow. Figs typically originate from warmer tropical regions that benefit from higher humidity, and to grow them well at home you need to recreate these conditions as closely as possible.

FICUS LYRATA
FIDDLE-LEAF FIG
▼

WHY GROW IT

Many figs have large, glossy leaves that are brilliantly bold and create a real tropical effect. Although in their natural jungle environment they can grow into a really large tree, a fig plant will be much better behaved when growing inside a living room, where you can keep it in check and prune to the required size or shape.

WHERE TO PUT IT

Find somewhere indoors that benefits from good light levels but avoids the midday sun and direct sunlight, which can burn and scorch the plant. Position well away from any radiators, doors or windows, which can cause unnecessary extremes of hot and cold.

HOW TO LOOK AFTER IT

When growing a fig as a house plant, the main thing to keep an eye on is watering. Too much water can cause the roots to rot, while too little water can cause the plant to suffer pretty similar die-back (the progressive death of twigs and branches), meaning that it's often difficult to tell what is going wrong. The best solution is to keep an eye on the compost. Once it has dried out fully, give the plant a generous drink and then leave it alone for at least a week. Misting the plant regularly can also help to keep the humidity high and the plant happy.

DO

Allow the plant to dry out completely before rewatering – this helps prevent it from becoming waterlogged

Keep an eye out for mealybug – this tends to be the main problem pest for figs

Pinch out the growing tips to encourage the fig to send out more sideshoots and produce a bushier, healthier plant

DON'T

Get the sap on your skin – figs have a latex-like sap that some people can be sensitive to

Keep it too close to a cold window or door – this can cause the plant to stress and stop growing

Repot it too often – figs almost prefer being slightly pot-bound

01

01. FICUS ELASTICA
RUBBER PLANT
A staple plant for most living rooms, other than the odd water and occasional feeding, the rubber plant really does just get on with it. Pinch out the top to encourage it to form a bushier plant.

02. FICUS BENJAMINA
BENJAMIN TREE
Much smaller leaves create a dense evergreen foliage that loves a sunny position away from direct light. The Benjamin tree is a lot softer and more restrained compared to its larger siblings.

02

MONSTERA DELICIOSA

SWISS CHEESE PLANT

Native to the rainforests of Mexico, this evergreen climber will give your home a lush, tropical feel. The Swiss cheese plant gets its name from the holes in its leaves, which resemble those found in Swiss cheese. As the plant matures, the holes will become larger and more prominent.

MONSTERA DELICIOSA
SWISS CHEESE PLANT
▶

NEED TO KNOW
—

SIZE
UP TO 8M (26FT)
(DON'T WORRY, IT
WON'T GET THIS BIG
INSIDE YOUR HOUSE)
—

LIGHT
PARTIAL SUN
—

SOIL TYPE
HOUSE PLANT
POTTING COMPOST
—

MOISTURE
MOIST BUT
WELL DRAINED
—

WHY GROW IT

In recent years, Swiss cheese plants have become immensely popular on Instagram, with their bold and impressive foliage making for a real statement plant. The unusual aerial roots add character and make the plant a great talking point, perhaps as a centrepiece in a living room.

WHERE TO PUT IT

Grow out of direct sunlight somewhere slightly shady: in the wild, the Swiss cheese plant naturally grows in dappled light, clinging to the trunks of large trees. It enjoys heading upwards, looking for light from above, so if you have a stairwell or an overhead window then this is ideal. Avoid growing it near a radiator or heat source that will scorch the leaves.

HOW TO LOOK AFTER IT

Ensure the plant is always kept moist. Good humidity is key, as it prefers to grow in a warm and wet environment. Although this isn't necessarily feasible in a small home, you can mist the foliage, which will help to create the same effect. The aerial roots can be pruned back if they begin to become intrusive or, ideally, you can simply push them back into the soil, which will help the plant look after itself.

DO

Mist the leaves regularly to recreate the humid conditions in which the plant would naturally grow

Put plants in a lukewarm shower to remove any dust and help wash off any pests that may be developing

Provide a structure within the pot for the plant to climb up

DON'T

Allow the plant to completely dry out – it prefers to be kept slightly damp

Grow in full sunlight – this can scorch the leaves and damage the plant

Worry if the plant begins to become too large – you can cut it back hard in the spring and it will bounce back

OTHERS TO TRY

—

MONSTERA DELICIOSA
'VARIEGATA' VARIEGATED
SWISS CHEESE PLANT

The variegated version has
become somewhat of an
international superstar, with
plants being slightly more difficult
to get hold of and much more
expensive. Despite the heavy
price tag, they prove well worth
the effort, producing large, glossy
leaves smudged with pure white.

UMBRELLA TREE

—

This is the easiest and most resilient of all the house plants I have ever grown. I have one nestled right by my sofa and, as I write this, I have suddenly realised that it has been at least a month since it last saw any water. Despite this level of neglect, it continues to thrive, and has done so for the last five years. For this reason alone, I believe every living room should have its own umbrella tree.

SCHEFFLERA
UMBRELLA TREE
▶

NEED TO KNOW

—

SIZE
UP TO 1.5M
(5FT) INDOORS

—

LIGHT
INDIRECT SUNLIGHT
OR SEMI-SHADE

—

SOIL TYPE
HOUSE PLANT
POTTING COMPOST

—

MOISTURE
MOIST BUT
WELL DRAINED

—

WHY GROW IT

Despite being difficult to grow outdoors, the umbrella tree makes a remarkably easy house plant. Its glossy, palmate foliage (the leaves fan out from a central point) makes it a brilliant tropical addition to a living room. The new leaves are a glorious lime-green, and they emerge throughout the year to replace the old, tired foliage.

WHERE TO PUT IT

In its natural habitat, the umbrella tree would grow into a huge tree – a real tropical rainforest giant. However, it will not reach this size in the home. Find somewhere that benefits from some light but which is not in direct sun – a position in semi-shade would be ideal.

HOW TO LOOK AFTER IT

Most gardening books will tell you to water your umbrella tree regularly. However, you can afford to be a little forgetful. Feeding it once a month with a balanced house plant feed will help to keep the foliage looking fresh and lush. Remove any old, tatty foliage and ensure that the plant doesn't sit in too much water.

DO

Strip any old, yellow leaves
back to the main stem

Spray the foliage with plant
invigorator to keep the plant
healthy and pest-free

Give it a lukewarm shower once
a month to remove any dust and keep
the plant looking fresh and shiny

DON'T

Overwater – just water it every few
weeks (if you do overwater, the
foliage can begin to turn yellow)

Grow it too near to a heat source
such as a radiator – this can cause the
foliage to burn and become crispy

Grow in full sun – a slightly
shady position is ideal

HOUSELEEK

———

Sempervivums are small, colourful, fleshy rosettes that form a ground-hugging mound over time. The individual rosettes come in a variety of colours, including yellow, red and purple, as well as green. Depending on the species they can be hairy or glossy, rounded or pointed. In summer, mature rosettes will produce a stem of flowers that look like tiny stars.

SEMPERVIVUM

HOUSELEEK

▼

—

SIZE
UP TO 20CM
(7.8IN) HIGH

—

LIGHT
FULL SUN

—

SOIL TYPE
SANDY

—

MOISTURE
WELL DRAINED

—

VARIETIES
S. tectorum, common
houseleek; *S. arachnoides*,
cobweb houseleek;
S. calcareum 'Mrs
Giuseppi', houseleek

WHY GROW IT

The name 'houseleek' comes from the fact that these plants were traditionally grown on roofs as an insurance policy against lightning strikes. They have also been used to ward off everything from witchcraft to the plague. Of greater relevance today, the Latin name *Sempervivum* translates as 'forever alive', which reflects the fact that these stylish plants thrive with virtually no maintenance.

WHERE TO PUT IT

As long as they're in full sun and well-drained soil, Sempervivums can be grown practically anywhere, including beds (where they make a good edging plant), rockeries and even crevices in walls. Make them a feature by planting in pots, troughs and sinks. They are also perfect candidates for vertical planting and green roofs. They can be grown indoors, but they need plenty of light.

HOW TO LOOK AFTER IT

Sempervivums need poor, gritty soil with good drainage and full sun. In the garden, add plenty of grit or sand to the planting hole and ensure your plant will receive maximum sunlight. In containers, make sure that there are adequate drainage holes, and layer crocks at the bottom before planting in a mix of grit, sand and compost and placing in a hot, dry position.

DO

Plant them in gritty soil and add plenty of sand to your compost mix

Try mixing varieties for an interesting, textured display

Be creative with your planting and think about using quirky containers

DON'T

Grow in damp areas – they dislike being wet and cold

Plant in areas where taller plants will shade and overwhelm them

Overwater or overfeed – they are tough plants that can take a little neglect

THREE TO TRY

01

01. *SEMPERVIVUM TECTORUM*
COMMON HOUSELEEK
Green/purple and vigorous.

02. *SEMPERVIVUM ARACHNOIDEUM*
COBWEB HOUSELEEK
This houseleek is covered in a web
of fine white hairs.

03. *SEMPERVIVUM CALCAREUM*
'MRS GIUSEPPI'
These relatively large rosettes have
stunning red tips.

02

03

PEACE LILY

The peace lily is reliable, easy and beautiful – the perfect combination for any plant. Its easy-to-grow nature makes it the ideal starter plant for anyone looking for their very first house plant, or perfect as a gift that will give continual enjoyment for years to come.

SPATHIPHYLLUM
WALLISII
PEACE LILY
▶

NEED TO KNOW
—

SIZE
UP TO 50cm
(20in) TALL
—

LIGHT
PARTIAL SHADE
—

SOIL TYPE
HOUSE PLANT
POTTING COMPOST
—

MOISTURE
MOIST BUT
WELL DRAINED
—

WHY GROW IT
The glossy, evergreen foliage provides a perfect base for the beautifully crisp, pure-white spathes (sheaths) of the flowers. Not only does the peace lily bring greenery indoors, but it can enhance any room.

WHERE TO PUT IT
Although this plant will grow just about anywhere inside, find somewhere in your home with good light levels, but not in direct sunshine, which can scorch and burn the leaves. The plant will tolerate a very shady location, but this will inhibit flowering. Make sure you don't grow it too close to a radiator or heat source, as this can burn the plant.

HOW TO LOOK AFTER IT
Try not to give it too much attention. In the case of the peace lily, neglect can actually lead to a stronger plant. Don't give it too much fertiliser or too much water. Cut back the faded flowers once they have done their thing, as the more you deadhead, the more flowers you will receive. The plant will benefit from having a lukewarm shower every few months. This serves to wash the leaves and water the plant at the same time.

DO

Allow the plant to dry out completely before rewatering – stressing the plant slightly in this way can help it to produce more flowers

Keep it away from windows during cold weather, as it could be caught by frosts through the glass

Plant it in a larger pot once the roots begin to completely fill the original pot

DON'T

Overwater or leave the plant sitting in water – this is the biggest killer of house plants, especially peace lilies

Grow in direct sunlight – although they need bright light to produce flowers, direct sunlight can scorch the leaves

Water with cold water – this can shock the plant

AIR PLANT

Air plants are some of the most peculiar, fun and extraordinary plants you could possibly hope to grow. These alien-like house guests defy the rules that most plants obey, as they literally grow in mid-air without any soil – yes, seriously! Epiphytic plants have adapted to grow out of the soil; instead, they cling to the branches of large tropical trees and collect their moisture from the air.

TILLANDSIA

AIR PLANT

▼

SIZE

CAN TRAIL UP

TO 1ᴍ (3ꜰᴛ)

—

LIGHT

FULL SUN TO

DAPPLED SHADE

—

SOIL TYPE

NO SOIL REQUIRED

—

MOISTURE

MOIST BUT

WELL DRAINED

—

VARIETIES

T. xerographica,

king of air plants;

T. usneoides,

Spanish moss

WHY GROW IT

Their fine, silvery foliage creates a tropical effect, yet despite their confusing and unusual appearance, air plants are in fact very easy to grow. These plants are resilient and difficult to kill, and are sure to attract attention from friends and family. And if you do want to share it with a friend, you can easily tear off and give away part of the plant.

WHERE TO PUT IT

Air plants love a high-humidity atmosphere – avoid growing them anywhere too sunny or with dry heat. The best place to grow them can actually be in a bathroom close to a window, as the humidity from the shower each day will keep the plants well watered. Grow in good light but avoid direct sunlight.

HOW TO LOOK AFTER IT

Air plants take in moisture through their fine foliage, so ensure that you mist them regularly. If the plants do dry out, you can dunk them in water to rehydrate them quickly. Where possible, use rainwater instead of tap water, as this can be softer on the foliage. Try to keep the plants constantly warm and away from any cold areas. If the temperature drops below 12 degrees Celsius reduce watering, as it can take the plants longer to dry out.

DO

Provide support for the plants to grow on, be it some old bark or cork, or even just by hanging them from a wall

Mist regularly to keep the plants well hydrated

Grow in the bathroom – the humidity from the shower will perfectly mimic the conditions the plant would naturally experience in a tropical rainforest

DON'T

Allow the plants to sit in moisture for too long – they like to be airy and light, as the name suggests

Let the plants dry out completely – if you do, dunk them quickly in a bucket of water and then allow them to dry out fully afterwards

Restrict ventilation – good aeration around the plants is key to ensure they don't rot

TILLANDSIA
TWO TO TRY

01

02

INDEX